Paper Art Workshop

CELEBRATING BABY

Personalized Projects for Moms, Memories, & Gear

QUARRY BOOKS

jennifer francis bitto, linda blinn,
jenn mason [THE MIXED MEDIUMS]

First published in the United States of America by
Quarry Books, a member of
Quayside Publishing Group
33 Commercial Street
Gloucester, Massachusetts 01930-5089
Telephone: (978) 282-9590
Fax: (978) 283-2742
www.rockpub.com

Library of Congress Cataloging-in-Publication Data
Bitto, Jennifer Francis.
    Celebrating baby : personalized projects for moms, memories, and gear / Jennifer Francis
Bitto, Linda Blinn, Jenn Mason.
        p.   cm. — (Paper art workshop)
    ISBN 1-59253-263-2 (pbk.)
    1. Handicraft. 2. Paper work. 3. Infants' supplies. I. Blinn, Linda. II. Mason, Jenn. III.
Title. IV. Series.

TT157.B554 2006
745.54—dc22   2006018998
                                                                               CIP

ISBN-13: 978-1-59253-263-6
ISBN-10: 1-59253-263-2

10 9 8 7 6 5 4 3 2 1

Design: Yee Design
Templates and Illustrations: Jenn Mason
Photography: Allan Penn

Printed in Singapore

CONTENTS

INTRODUCTION

We've been delighted to see the sudden injection of style into today's baby industry. We've witnessed design styles from ruffian to rockstar and ruffles to retro, all suited for little dudes, divas, prepsters, and hippies. It seems that we parents and aunts and uncles want to relive our own childhoods and share a slice of that history, specifically all the fun designs and themes that we've grown up with. And in this spirit, we have interpreted our memories and style influences to create our own collection of handmade baby accoutrements.

Paper art seemed the perfect medium to use to interpret these themes and create baby gear and décor that put a twist on traditional, show a sense of humor, and use playful retro references. Paper is easy and fun to work with and offers limitless options for colors and themes. Choose any of these ideas and interpret it your way. Go vintage, whimsical, kitschy—or even sweet—and give it a hip twist.

These projects were designed to give a personalized and one-of-a-kind touch to baby décor, gear, and gifts. In the first chapter, Great Expectations, you'll find art to decorate the nursery, ideas for fanciful showers, and a range of clever baby journals and albums. Subsequent chapters feature announcements and keepsakes and we show you how to travel easily and in style. And in each chapter you will find a section called Leftovers. Far from a reheated casserole, our Leftovers show you what can be done with the scraps and bits left over from several of these projects.

We represent the entire motherhood spectrum. Jenn Mason has faux twins: her six- and seven-year-old daughters differ only in size. Jennifer Francis Bitto is a mother-to-be (at some point in time) and Linda Blinn is a grandmother who knows that this is the real reason to have kids. So, grab your retro toys, your vintage children's books, your Smurf collection, and come with us on creative adventures from the best paper stores to architectural salvage companies. We will tell you about our favorite sources, techniques, and shortcuts, and why we are inspired by something as simple as a baby's bib or as sophisticated as a chandelier. We are happy you joined us—and be sure to send us a baby announcement!

Tools and Supplies

This is a wish list of art supplies. We don't actually have all of these materials at any point in time or enough room to accommodate such an all-inclusive assortment if we did. Your collection of art supplies will evolve over time as you experiment with various techniques and products. Shop smart, use coupons, compare prices, and check out materials on various websites. You might want to buy certain items in bulk with friends. It is amazing what we can create with even a moderate amount of materials. Some of our best projects happen when we "make do."

Basic Tool Kit

The Basic Tool Kit appears throughout the book. It contains the fundamental tools you will need to make the featured projects.

- bone folder
- craft knife
- hole punch
- metal-edge ruler
- scissors
- stylus

Extras

Keep this list handy whenever you are shopping for art supplies. Like basic staples in the kitchen pantry, a collection of these items will ensure that you can serve up some art at a moment's notice.

ADHESIVES

- clear glaze
- decoupage medium
- Diamond Glaze
- double-sided tape
- extra-strength glue
- foam adhesive squares
- gel medium
- gesso
- glue dots
- glue stick
- hook and loop tape (such as Velcro)
- mounting foam tape
- removable tape
- spray adhesive
- white glue

HARDWARE

- binder clips
- brads
- circle punch
- corner-rounding punch
- decorative punches
- decorative-edge scissors
- die-cut system with dies
- eyelets and eyelet setter
- grommet setter
- hammer
- hole punch (heavy duty)
- needle-nose pliers
- paper cutter
- rubber bands
- snaps and setter
- staples and stapler

EMBELLISHMENTS

- alphabet stickers
- buttons
- collage items (such as brass charms, magnetic clips, mailbox stickers, old rulers, or wooden letters)
- decorative tape
- epoxy stickers
- glitter
- photo corners
- ribbon
- rickrack
- round metal-rimmed paper tags
- rubber stamps
- rub-on letters, words, and designs
- stickers
- waxed string or twine

PAPER

- acetate transparency
- alphabet stickers
- chipboard letters and numbers
- contact paper
- decorative papers (such as wrapping paper or scrapbook paper)
- die-cut letters and shapes
- envelopes
- foam board (such as Fome-Cor)
- mat board
- old book pages
- plain-colored card stock
- poster board
- tags
- tissue paper
- vellum
- vintage papers and ephemera
- watercolor paper

FOR ADDING COLOR

- acrylic glaze
- acrylic paint
- black ink pen
- felt-tip markers
- foam brushes and wedges
- ink stamping pads
- metallic foil pens
- metallic paint
- paintbrushes
- spray paint
- watercolor paint
- watercolor pencils

Items You'll Need to Make These Specific Projects

- adhesive-backed CD envelope
- baby clothing
- beading wire
- beads (crimp, silver spacer, round, and crystal)
- black Bristol board
- buttons (shank style, vintage buttons in various colors)
- cardboard tube
- chandelier
- chandelier crystals
- chenille fabric
- child-sized flatware and dinnerware
- chopsticks
- clear plastic tubing
- clock hands
- clothlike table cover
- coin holders
- color wheel
- colored portfolios
- cotton fabric paper
- craft iron
- embossing powder (thick)
- empty mint tin
- gift bags
- jump rings
- large-format book to alter
- Lucite purse handle
- luggage tags (leather, plastic, or Lucite)
- metal frame
- metal label holder
- old baby mobile
- paint chips
- painting canvas
- paper board suitcase
- papier-mâché boxes
- paper party noisemakers
- photo turns
- pie template
- plastic forks and spoons
- plastic pouch
- quilt batting
- round clock (new or used)
- sewing machine
- silicone craft sheet
- small key chain
- stir sticks
- towel
- vintage or black-and-white photographs
- water mister bottle
- wooden blocks measuring $1/2$" (1.3 cm)
- wooden frame
- wooden hearts and letters
- zipper

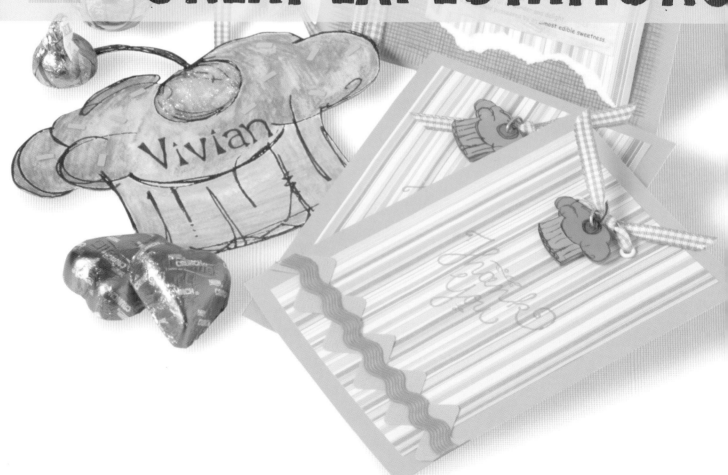

GREAT EXPECTATIONS

Noothing says baby like the ABCs. In this chapter, we see alphabet letters transform babyhood motifs and become novel nursery décor and accessories. They dance across a colorful collage, move on a mobile, boldly appear on flash cards, and serve up some tasty wall art.

Making the decision to have a child—it's momentous.

It is to decide forever to have your heart go walking outside your body.

—ELIZABETH STONE

Currently, nursery décor, clothing, and baby gear often reflect the parents' personal taste and this often includes motifs from their own childhood. Our paper frames show how one technique can be interpreted in a variety of these styles: retro, vintage, and western. And, with traditional colors now pairing with retro reds, 1950s turquoise, earthy browns, and every shade of green, it has never been easier to execute your own personal vision of baby style.

This "anything goes" attitude definitely influences the options when planning baby showers. In this chapter, two diverse approaches are offered. The sweet and playful cupcake shower and the sophisticated Asian-inspired shower offer a world of inspiration on invitations, goody bags, and decorations.

When Mom-to-be has time for some reflective moments, a handmade personal journal will be just the thing to record memories of the nine months of pregnancy along with her wishes and dreams for the baby.

The Leftovers will have you thinking twice before tossing all the scraps you accumulate from making the projects. These easy, breezy, fast, and functional ideas are intended to be simple and fun. If you are new to the world of paper and mixed-media art, you might even want to start with the simple techniques outlined in Leftovers and then move on to other projects in the chapter.

Repurposed Mobile

MATERIALS

- purchased baby mobile
- square stretched canvases
- handmade paper
- vintage book pages
- card stock
- acrylic glazes or thinned acrylic paints
- ribbon, 1" (2.5 cm) and $^1/_4$" (6 mm) wide
- black drawing pen
- nail heads
- soft gel (matte)
- $^1/_2$" (1.3 cm) grommet
- screw eye hooks
- decorative pins (optional)

TOOLS

- basic tool kit (see page 10)
- long-reach $^1/_2$" (1.3 cm) circle punch
- paintbrush
- grommet setter
- hammer
- template (see page 103)

We may agree that having a mobile is a nursery necessity, but we also agree that this rotating music box can also be a quintessential piece of art in baby's bedroom. Covered in handmade paper, and decorated with simple shapes cut from glazed vintage book pages (see templates on page 103), these miniature canvases hang with the greatest of ease. The secret is to repurpose an existing mobile where all the work of balancing and general construction has been done for you. The canvases can be quickly transferred to baby's wall once the mobile has been outgrown.

Making the Canvases

INSTRUCTIONS

1 Paint the front and sides of the canvases with the main glaze color. Let dry.

2 Use the long-reach punch to make evenly spaced circles out of a piece of card stock cut to the same size as the canvas.

3 Use the punched card stock as a stencil and paint polka dots on the front of each canvas using a second glaze color. Let dry.

4 Glaze the vintage book pages, let dry, and cut out the desired shapes (see template on page 103). Use soft gel to attach the shapes to the canvases.

5 Loosely outline the shapes with a black drawing pen.

6 Cut strips of the glazed paper to cover the edges of the canvases. Adhere the strips with soft gel.

7 Cover the backs of the canvases with handmade paper and add the screw eye hook to the top corner about 1" (2.5 cm) from the top.

8 Tie four bows and attach each one to the top, front corner of each canvas with glue or decorative pins.

Studio Tip

Pink or blue? Traditionally, we think of pink for girls and blue for boys, but did you know that only recently, circa 1950, did this gender color specification occur? Up until that time, pink—a shade of red—was thought of as masculine—representing war, blood, courage, and passion. Blue was perceived as the daintier color—signifying the sky, heavens, and all things ethereal and feminine.

Making the Mobile

1 Start by taking apart the hanging apparatus for the mobile. Under all the decorations should be a basic ring shape, from which each canvas will hang.

2 Use soft gel to attach torn strips of handmade paper to the main arm of the mobile and the ring shape. Let dry.

3 Cut and adhere pieces of the glazed book pages used on the canvases to cover the music box component.

4 Cut two pieces of the 1" (2.5 cm) ribbon to the length needed for your ring to hang from the music box component plus 2" (5.1 cm).

5 Cross the two ribbon pieces perpendicularly at their center points and secure with the grommet using a craft knife to make the opening in the ribbon.

6 Lay these ribbons evenly over the ring shape. Fold the end of one ribbon under ¼" (6 mm). Pull the ribbon under and up through the ring until it loops around and touches itself just above the ring. Secure it with a nail head.

Shopping Tip

You can certainly alter a new mobile, but if you're up for a treasure hunt, try perusing your local secondhand stores. The mobile used in this project was unearthed at a local store for under $2! On your way home, check out the used bookstore for old children's books. Text-covered pages were used for the majority of the project, but a small illustration was featured on the front of the music box component. Look for interesting books that match the theme of the baby's room.

Always give a book a sniff test. If it smells moldy, leave it on the shelf! Also check for brittleness. If a book is particularly old, make sure the pages aren't too fragile or they won't stand up to painting, cutting, bending, and gluing.

These simple shapes can be changed to fit any theme. Using a fine-point black pen and a loose touch, create a whimsical outline by tracing around each shape twice.

7 Repeat for the other three ends, keeping the ribbon even.

8 Measure the distance you want the canvases to hang from the ring. Cut four pieces of ¹/₄" (6 mm) ribbon this measurement plus 3" (7.6 cm).

9 Attach the end of one of these ribbons with a nail head to the 1" (2.5 cm) ribbon on the mobile, just above the existing nail head.

10 Thread the bottom of this ribbon up through the screw eye on the back of one canvas so that the ribbon overlaps about 1¹/₄" (3.1 cm) and secure with a nail head. Repeat steps 8 and 9 for the other three canvases.

11 Assemble the mobile.

Studio Tip

Because these flash cards are easy to size up or down, they become room décor accents as well as learning tools.

- Clip four or five cards around the top of a lamp shade with tiny clothespins.
- Attach cards to a cord with mini clothespins and use as a window valance.
- Use multiple copies as a wall border.
- Hang from a mobile or ceiling light.
- Add a ribbon loop to the top and place on a doorknob.
- String across the top of a mirror.

- Resize and reuse your flash cards

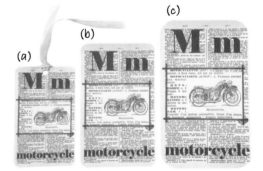

(a) Reduce a set of cards size to 50 percent and make a deck.

(b) Reduce the size to 60 percent for original gift tags.

(c) Reduce the size to 65 percent for an all-occasion card.

MATERIALS

- card stock or poster board
- rub-on letters
- chipboard letters
- die-cut letters
- wooden letters
- alphabet stickers
- wooden hearts
- ribbon or twill
- linen twine
- old French dictionary (or clip art, page 117)
- cotton fabric paper
- scrapbook paper
- tissue paper
- zipper
- glue stick
- adhesive dots
- ink pads
- white acrylic paint
- black solvent ink stamp
- double-sided tape
- foam board (such as Fome-Cor)

Optional:

- small key chain
- papier-mâché box
- spray paint

TOOLS

- basic tool kit (see page 10)
- round corner punch
- alphabet die-cut system

TRÈS BON

French Flash Cards

Take the alphabet to a higher level of learning and gather some tips on the ABCs of decorating a child's room at the same time. We expanded and super-sized the concept of flash cards as a traditional learning tool and transformed them into decorative accents, perfect for the nursery.

A vintage French dictionary is the starting point for this set of flash cards. The pages have line drawings of objects and animals that can be enlarged to fit the proportion of the cards. Depending on your choice of materials, this project adapts to any nursery theme: 1950s pink poodles, animal prints, airplanes, or sentimental hearts. If you prefer bright, primary colors, consider going Hawaiian (S is for surf) or South of the Border (P is for piñata). Make the cards personal with photos of family instead of graphics: D for Dad, M for Mom, and first name initials for siblings, aunts, uncles, and cousins.

INSTRUCTIONS

The card is composed of four elements: a background page, a line drawing of an object from a French dictionary, a letter representing the first letter of the object, and the name of the object. The card can be either computer generated and printed on card stock or made by collaging the various elements onto card stock or poster board.

❶ Cut card stock or poster board to measure $5^{3}/_{4}" \times 9^{1}/_{4}"$ (14.6 × 23.5 cm).

❷ Scan or color copy the selected old dictionary pages.

❸ Glue the dictionary page to the card stock or poster board and round the corners with a punch.

❹ Make an enlarged copy of the object or animal from the dictionary page and place it in the middle of the flash card.

❺ Add uppercase and lowercase letters above the object.

❻ Spell out the name of the object beneath it using rub-on letters or stickers or computer-generated fonts.

VARIATIONS ON A THEME

Recalling the famous pink poodle motif of the 1950s, this card also lets the toddler pull a pink P out of a pocket.

Zebra stripes reinforce the Z sound while the zipper adds a hands-on opportunity to practice zzzzzipping.

Easy enough for a youngster to make, this flying flash card requires just a little help with cutting, pasting, and printing letters.

Reminiscent of a valentine, this card announces that H is for heart (and offers a hearty supply of polka dots.)

Sweetie Pie Frame

Start little ones early with spelling and vocabulary. Of course, these terms are not necessarily the ones you will find in a dictionary right off the shelf. We've taken a little artistic license and created our own words with corresponding meanings. Using the language of endearment we so often verbalize with our babies, we were inspired to create artwork and definitions in true "Mixed Medium" style. Photocopy and size the pie imagery on page 112 to your desired format. Can't get enough of this idea? You'll also find clip art for a love bug and cupcake with suggested definitions (on pages 111–112) to fill the walls in your baby's nursery.

INSTRUCTIONS

1 Paint a 12" × 12" (30.5 × 30.5 cm) wooden frame with acrylic paint. Add polka dots with another color of paint. Rub a third color of paint on the edges using a foam brush.

2 Stamp the flatware image repeatedly with a watermark ink pad on an 11" × 11" (27.9 × 27.9 cm) paper panel to create a background pattern. To create the place mat, trim a 9^1/$_2$" × 7^1/$_4$" (24.1 × 18.4 cm) piece of card stock with decorative scallop-edge scissors. Punch holes along the edges in each scallop.

3 Center and glue the place mat panel to the stamped paper panel. Then center and glue both to a panel measuring 12" × 12" (30.5 × 30.5 cm). Place the layered panels in the frame.

4 Gently break off one end of two stir rods and paint them with acrylic paint. Using a dry brush, cover the surfaces with white paint. Add the words *noun. 1: a little squirt/capable of stealing hearts…* to the sticks with rub-on letters.

5 Decoupage colored tissue paper to a small saucer or plate. Paint the fork, knife, and spoon with gesso. Decoupage the flatware with white tissue paper.

6 Photocopy and size the pie imagery from page 112. Color with watercolor pencils and cut out.

7 Computer generate *cute enough to eat* for the fork tines. Sponge the saying with ink. Tuck the strip of paper into the fork tines and secure with glue.

8 Adhere the plate to the place mat using strong adhesive. Mount the pie to the plate using foam tape.

MATERIALS

- wooden frame measuring 12" × 12" (30.5 × 30.5 cm)
- child's flatware (fork, knife, and spoon)
- plastic saucer or small plate
- stir rods
- die-cut letters in a few different fonts
- rub-on letters
- ribbon
- acrylic paint
- gesso
- watercolor pencils
- tissue paper
- decorative paper
- card stock
- white glue
- strong adhesive (such as GOOP)
- foam tape
- decoupage medium or soft acrylic gel
- watermark ink
- clear ink pad
- blue ink pad
- thick embossing enamel

TOOLS

- basic tool kit (see page 10)
- flatware rubber stamp
- foam brush
- decorative scallop-edge scissors
- pie template (see page 112)

9 Fold a piece of decorative paper for a napkin and glue to the place mat. Tie the fork to the napkin with a ribbon. Tie the knife and spoon to the place mat with ribbons.

10 Paint die-cut letters that spell out *Sweetie Pie* with acrylic paint. When dry, sponge with clear ink. Emboss the surface with two layers of thick embossing enamel. Affix the embossed letters to the artwork.

Hanging Paper Frames

MATERIALS

- photo
- card stock
- decorative paper
- acetate
- brads
- ribbon measuring 36" to 40" (91.4 to 101.6 cm) in length

TOOLS

- basic tool kit (see page 10)
- decorative-edge scissors

This project was specially designed to give us an opportunity to use more of our favorite studio supply—paper! Using paper for construction, paper for decoration and, even "clear" paper (a.k.a. acetate) for the window, this frame gets that little extra something with decorative-edge scissors and a touch of beautiful ribbon. There are so many possibilities for this project. By just changing the paper, ribbon, or accessories, you achieve a completely different look (see the variations on pages 26–27). Try making small versions for party favors or ornaments, or make multiples to showcase baby's family tree.

INSTRUCTIONS

1 Cut out two sheets of card stock approximately 3" to 4" (7.6 to 10.2 cm) bigger than the width and length of the photograph. Use decorative-edge scissors if desired. Set one card stock aside for the frame backing.

2 Adhere decorative paper or vellum to the other piece of card stock, which will become the frame front. Trim if necessary.

3 Cut another piece of coordinating decorative paper 1" (2.5 cm) longer and wider than the photo. Center this on the back side of the frame front.

4 Use a craft knife and a metal-edge ruler to cut an X in the frame slightly smaller than the dimension of the picture.

5 With the frame front faceup, turn, peel, or fold back the inside flaps created by cutting the X (see photo). Secure the corners with brads, eyelets, or glue (see variations on pages 26–27).

6 Glue acetate to the back side of the frame front to create a window.

7 Tie a bow in the center of the ribbon and glue the ends to the back side of the frame front, making sure they don't show through the acetate window.

8 Glue the frame backing to the frame front along the bottom and sides. Slip in the photo.

VARIATIONS ON A THEME

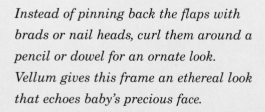

Instead of pinning back the flaps with brads or nail heads, curl them around a pencil or dowel for an ornate look. Vellum gives this frame an ethereal look that echoes baby's precious face.

Consider the photo when choosing your papers. A baby picture of this daddy calls for retro '70s-inspired patterned paper. Strips of paper embellish the opening and reinforce the strong linear feel of the paper.

It's the mix—not the match—in this version, which combines real leather, paper painted to look like denim, and a photocopy of antique lace. To create the denim look, we painted a piece of card stock with indigo blue glaze, laid cheesecloth on the wet glaze, and then ran a brayer over the top to create the fiber pattern. Remove the cheesecloth and voilà!

Traditional elements get an updated look in this textural frame crafted from anaglyptic wallpaper with a touch of blue toile. Distressed pink paper, wee flowers, and tiny rhinestones give it the ultimate shabby chic makeover.

Great Expectations | **27**

ABC Canvas

Clearly the Mixed Mediums have a thing for letters and text. We just can't get enough of this kind of wall art! In this project, the alphabet has swallowed a rainbow and been transformed through paint, stencils, and whimsical embellishments.

Think beyond *B is for Ball* or *C is for Cat*. Search your stash of supplies to help determine which letters could include a unique element. The letter *K* is crafted from a key. The letter *H* has just a trace of a heart hanging through the center. *V* is for violet, while *L* is for ladybug. Use a variety of chipboard letters, rub-ons, computer fonts, or stencils to personalize your ABC collage.

Applications such as crackle medium or molding paste add terrific textural surfaces perfect for little fingers exploring the shapes of these letters. Believe it or not, only six paint colors were used on this canvas. But by mixing the colors and lightening or darkening the shades, new hues were achieved but remain true to the same color family. Match your colors of paint with the baby's nursery décor and experiment with fonts—perhaps you will prefer using just one or two.

INSTRUCTIONS

1 Paint the stretched canvas with two coats of gesso.

2 Using a ruler and a pencil, divide the canvas into blocks for each letter or group of letters. This canvas was divided into twenty-five sections.

3 Mask the division lines with painter's tape and begin painting each block. Mix the acrylic paint with molding paste until it looks like frosting. Use the negative and positive space created by chipboard letters to add dimension to some blocks. Paint chipboard letters and add polka dots with the handle end of a paintbrush. A rubber comb drawn through wet paint makes interesting textures too. Paint crackling medium onto the canvas. Let dry until tacky. Paint over the crackling medium, allowing cracks to form and split the paint.

4 Computer generate large letters and cut them out. Trace them onto decorative papers or ephemera for patterned letters. Apply them to the painted canvas with decoupage medium. Hot-glue embellishments to the letters for a personalized look. Use a permanent marker and stencils to draw letters onto the painted blocks.

MATERIALS

- stretched canvas measuring 16" × 20" (40.6 × 50.8 cm)
- chipboard letters in a variety of fonts and sizes
- rub-on letters
- decorative paper, sheet music, old ledger pages, or other ephemera
- velvet flower
- felt
- skeleton key
- ladybug charm
- cloth tag
- buckle
- ribbon
- gesso
- acrylic paint
- crackling medium
- decoupage medium
- molding paste
- hot glue gun and glue

TOOLS

- basic tool kit (see page 10)
- pencil
- permanent marker
- paintbrush
- foam brushes
- rubber comb
- stencils
- painter's tape
- computer (optional)

5 Create the letter O using a decorative buckle. Thread satin ribbon through the buckle and secure with decoupage medium. Use hot glue to anchor the buckle to the canvas and wrap the end of the ribbon around the frame and secure on the back with more glue.

6 Wrap the canvas frame with a pretty ribbon or add a solid painted edge to finish it. Don't forget to sign and date your canvas.

Studio Tip

A Quick History of Decoupage

The art of decoupage is the simple technique of cutting and pasting images onto furniture or home accessories to create the illusion of a painted motif. Originally called a poor man's art, decoupage was used when a household could not afford to pay an artisan to paint their home or furniture. With multiple coats of lacquer or varnish over intricately cut images, wonderfully elegant results could be attained.

Come Celebrate
The Little
Cupcake

Cupcake: (cŭp' cāk). Noun
1. a small tyke full of wonder and delight.
2. a small child possessed by an almost edible sweetness.

Cupcake Shower

The little cupcake is on her way and it's time for a party. Celebrate the mom-to-be and her baby with something sweet—cupcakes, of course! This festive motif can grace the invitations, party favors, and even name tags. You can size the cupcake up or down depending on your needs. We used it with shrink plastic in a variety of sizes to make durable charms for the invites, thank-you notes, and goody bags. And yes—little boys can be cupcakes too; just change the colors and you're ready to party!

MATERIALS

- shrink plastic
- card stock
- mesh paper
- decorative paper
- brads
- eyelets
- ribbon
- acrylic paints
- pigment inks
- orange paper shreds
- Diamond Glaze
- thin wire
- jump rings
- rubber stamp
- white paper
- watercolor pencils
- ultrafine glitter
- pin closure for a name tag
- cellophane bags
- candies

TOOLS

- basic tool kit (see page 10)
- paintbrush
- black permanent marker
- light box (optional)
- eyelet setter
- decorative hole punch
- decorative-edge scissors
- cupcake image (see page 112)

Making the Invitation

INSTRUCTIONS

1 Fold a piece of orange card stock into a 5" × 5" (12.7 × 12.7 cm) square card. Trim a piece of pink mesh paper to fit the front of the card. Cut a 3" × 4 1/2" (7.6 × 11.4 cm) strip of decorative paper and tear the bottom.

2 Trace the cupcake (see page 112) onto the torn panel with a black marker using a light box or by holding it up to a window. Adhere to the front of the card with two pink brads.

3 Trace the cupcake again onto shrink plastic with a black permanent marker. Color with acrylic paints. Cut out and punch a hole through the cherry. Shrink according to the manufacturer's instructions.

4 Computer generate *Come Celebrate the Little Cupcake* and the cupcake definition. Cut out the greeting in a tag shape and sponge with coordinating pigment inks. Cut out the definition and sponge in the same manner.

5 Tie ribbons around the front panel of the card, threading the greeting, and tie knots at the top of the card. Attach the shrink plastic cupcake to the tag with a jump ring.

6 Glue the cupcake definition to the bottom of the torn decorative panel.

Making the Goody Bag

1 Trace the cupcake (see page 112) onto shrink plastic with a black permanent marker.

2 Color with acrylic paints. When dry, handwrite a guest's name with a black permanent marker.

3 Punch a hole through the cherry and cut out. Shrink according to the manufacturer's instructions.

4 When cool, add Diamond Glaze to the cherry.

5 Fill a cellophane bag with orange paper shreds and add chocolate candies. Tie it closed with ribbons and attach the shrink plastic cupcake with thin wire.

Making the Thank-You Notes

INSTRUCTIONS

1 Fold a piece of orange card stock into a $3^{1}/_{2}$" × 5" (8.9 × 12.7 cm) card. Trim a piece of decorative paper to fit the front of the card.

2 Trim a pink card stock strip with decorative-edge scissors. Glue to the front of the card. Layer an orange piece of rickrack ribbon on the card stock strip.

3 Trace the cupcake (see page 112) onto shrink plastic with a black permanent marker.

4 Color with acrylic paints. Punch a hole through the cherry and cut out. Shrink according to the manufacturer's instructions.

5 Punch two holes in the top of the card. Set the holes with white eyelets.

6 Thread the eyelets with ribbon and tie into a knot. Secure the shrink plastic cupcake charm to the knot with a jump ring.

7 Stamp the sentiment on the front of the card with pigment ink.

Making the Name Tag

INSTRUCTIONS

1 Trace the cupcake (see page 112) onto white paper with a black permanent marker using a light box or by holding it up to a window. Color with water-color pencils, then lightly paint over it with a wet paintbrush. Handwrite a guest's name on the cupcake and cut out.

2 Glue to the pink card stock and cut out again. Attach a pin closure to the back of the cupcake.

3 Punch out small rectangles of orange card stock with a decorative hole punch. Glue to the cupcake for confetti sprinkles.

4 Apply Diamond Glaze and ultrafine glitter to the cherry.

Studio Tip

Thank-you notes made in the theme of the shower are a gift for any expecting mom. Make them when you're creating the invitations using leftover papers and charms. Present them after the party and you, too, will be showered with gratitude.

A heat gun or toaster oven is perfect for shrinking these little charms. We put them on a piece of brown paper bag while they shrank and used a bamboo skewer to help maneuver them while they were warm.

Chinese Shower

If you are looking for a unique theme for a baby shower, try this one—it's easy to cater, fun to decorate, and definitively memorable. Small paper lanterns can serve as place cards or as food placards for the buffet table. Take-out boxes with a contemporary twist go together quickly for favors. Even if you don't consider yourself a baker, you can easily whip up a batch of these paper fortune cookie invitations to give invitees a hint at what is to come. Beautifully wrapped chopstick holders will entice even the most reluctant eaters to try the dim sum. If you love this idea and want to use it for baby's first birthday, see page 80 for instructions on how to make matching party hats and party blowers for this Asian-inspired ensemble.

Making the Paper Lantern

INSTRUCTIONS

1. Glue two pieces of decorative paper back to back or use a piece of double-sided card stock. Cut into a 4" × 5 1/2" (10.2 × 14 cm) rectangle.

2. Fold in half with the right side facing out to make a 2" × 5 1/2" (5.1 × 14 cm) piece of paper. Make 1 1/2" (3.8 cm) cuts into the folded edge of the paper every 1/4" (6 mm).

3. Open the folded paper up and roll into a cylinder shape with the cuts running vertically and the right side facing out. Overlap the ends and adhere with a glue stick.

4. Cut two coordinating 12" (30.5 cm) strips of paper 3/8" (1 cm) and 1/2" (1.3 cm) wide. Adhere the narrow strip on top of the wide strip and cut in half. Glue the two pieces around the top and bottom of the lantern.

5. Punch two holes opposite each other along the top and add eyelets if desired. Cut a small flag shape out of paper, add a name, and adhere it to one end of the ribbon. Bend the flag back and forth for a rippled effect.

6. Thread ribbon through the holes and knot it to keep it in place.

MATERIALS

- card stock
- decorative paper
- eyelets
- ribbon
- chopsticks
- bamboo skewers
- brush markers
- foam adhesive squares
- glue stick

TOOLS

- basic tool kit (see page 10)
- eyelet setter
- template (see page 104)

Making the Take-Out Box

INSTRUCTIONS

1 Glue two pieces of decorative paper back to back or use double-sided card stock.

2 Trace the template (see page 104) onto the back of the paper and cut out. Score along the fold lines.

3 Punch out holes and add eyelets if desired.

4 Fold along the score lines to create the box shape, keeping the side flaps on the outside of the box. Lace ribbon through the holes to hold the box together.

Making the Fortune Cookie Invitation

INSTRUCTIONS

1 Glue two pieces of decorative paper back to back or use double-sided card stock.

2 Cut out a 5" (12.7 cm) circle and punch two holes on opposite sides of the circle ¹/₄" (6 mm) from the edge.

3 Slightly bend the circle in half with the eyelets at each end of the circle, making sure not to crease the circle.

4 Hold the right end of the fortune cookie in your right hand, and the left end of the fortune cookie in your left hand. Next, hold this half-circle (with the round part pointing up) at the midpoint perpendicular to the edge of the worktable. Pull down against the edge of the worktable with both hands, creating a crease in the fortune cookie circle, and gently bring the two eyeleted ends toward each other. Lace a ribbon through the eyelets to secure and adjust the cookie as necessary.

5 Print out or stamp the invitation information onto a slip of paper about ¹/₂" (1.3 cm) wide and slip it into the cookie.

Making the Chopstick Holder

INSTRUCTIONS

1 Cut a strip of card stock 2" × 12" (5.1 × 30.5 cm). With the card stock lying vertically, fold up the bottom 6³/₄" (17.1 cm) of the strip. Gently bend the top 1¹/₄" (3.2 cm) of the strip back down without making a sharp fold mark.

2 Cut 1" (2.5 cm) and 1¹/₂" (3.8 cm) strips of coordinating paper 12" (30.5 cm) long. Glue the narrow piece onto the wide piece. Cut this strip into two 4¹/₂" (11.4 cm) and one 3" (7.6 cm)-long pieces.

3 Wrap one of the long pieces around the folded card stock, secure the bent top piece underneath it, and glue the overlap.

4 Make a bow with the second long piece using the short piece as the center of the bow. Secure with glue and adhere over the folded and wrapped card stock with a foam adhesive square.

Studio Tip

The lanterns can be enlarged to use as centerpieces, or you can make smaller lanterns and hang them from bamboo skewers before inserting them into a flower arrangement. Also try using a brush marker to simulate Chinese brush lettering on your place cards.

wonder

i wonder what you'll look like

i wonder when you'll arrive

i wonder how much i'll love you

1

Pregnancy Journal

MATERIALS

- decorative paper
- card stock
- black Bristol board
- chipboard letters and numbers
- eyelets
- ribbon
- envelopes (regular, glassine, vellum)
- metal label holder
- fine-point marker
- brads
- photo turns
- glue stick

TOOLS

- basic tool kit (see page 10)
- heavy-duty hole punch
- large corner rounder punch
- eyelet setter
- decorative-edge scissors
- calendar template (see page 113)

Wonder who's coming? Wonder when he's coming? Wonder if the new arrival will be a boy or a girl? Keep track of your thoughts or make this gift of Wonder to an expectant mom. This lovely bound book can be filled with dreams, hopes, uncertainties, and expectations. Individual tabs, envelopes, and photo corners make this a useful gift that is appreciated for more than its inherent beauty. Interesting questions, quotes, and "keeping" places can be included to entice the new mom to wonder out loud. If you don't get to this project before baby arrives, consider altering it to be a baby book of memories or a book of personal parenting goals and desires.

Making the Cover

INSTRUCTIONS

1 Cut two pieces of Bristol board to $11^{1}/_{4}" \times 8"$ (28.6 × 20.3 cm) and two pieces $1^{1}/_{4}" \times 8"$ (3.2 × 20.3 cm).

2 Cut two pieces of decorative paper $2^{1}/_{2}" \times 9^{1}/_{2}"$ (6.4 × 24.1 cm) and two pieces $1^{3}/_{4}" \times 7^{1}/_{2}"$ (4.4 × 19.1 cm).

3 Lay one of the larger pieces of decorative paper facedown vertically on the work surface and cover with glue. Lay the 8" (20.3 cm) edge of the larger Bristol board over the left edge of the glued paper overlapping $^{1}/_{2}"$ (1.3 cm) and centered from top to bottom.

4 Lay one of the smaller boards next to this board leaving a $^{1}/_{8}"$ (3 mm) gap.

5 Miter the top and bottom right-hand corners of the decorative paper and fold up the excess paper. Cover this with one of the smaller pieces of decorative paper.

6 Repeat steps 2 through 5 for the other cover.

7 Make three evenly spaced holes down the center of the smaller sections of the cover using the heavy-duty hole punch.

Making the Month Pages

INSTRUCTIONS

1 Cut a 7¹/₂" (19.1 cm)-wide by 4¹/₂" (11.4 cm)-tall rectangle off the lower left corner of a 12" × 12" (30.5 × 30.5 cm) piece of card stock. Fold the bottom section of the paper up creating a 12" × 7¹/₂" (30.5 × 19.1 cm) piece of paper with a flap. Round the upper left corner of the flap and secure the right side with eyelet(s) to create a pocket.

2 Repeat eight more times to create nine pages.

3 Adhere chipboard numbers 1 through 9 to the papers.

Making the Wonder Pages and Inside Back Cover

INSTRUCTIONS

1 Cut four pieces of card stock measuring 12" × 7¹/₂" (30.5 × 19.1 cm).

2 To create the tabs, cut three pieces of card stock measuring 2¹/₂" × 3" (6.4 × 7.6 cm) and fold in half. Use a large corner rounder punch on the two folder corners. Layer with a ⁵/₈" × 2¹/₄" (1.6 × 5.7 cm) piece of card stock with two rounded corners.

3 On the first piece create a title page using chipboard letters, label holder, and brads or other embellishments.

4 On the second page, add a tab at the top right-hand corner and label it *I wonder what you'll look like.* Add card stock mats and photo turns for an ultrasound.

5 On the third page, add a tab halfway down the right-hand edge and label it *I wonder when you'll arrive*, and add a copy of the calendar (see page 113) and a card stock mat.

6 On the fourth page, add a tab at the bottom right-hand corner and label it *I wonder how much I'll love you*, and glue an envelope labeled *a letter from mommy* to the page.

7 For the inside back cover, cut off the top of a 6 1/2" (16.5 cm) square vellum envelope and glue it to the left side. Add a small glassine envelope filled with handmade photo corners (see Leftovers on page 73) to the right-hand side of the cover.

Putting It All Together

INSTRUCTIONS

1 Use one of the covers as a guide to punch the rest of the holes in the inside pages.

2 Line up all the pages and lace the book together with the covers in a pamphlet stitch. Pull a piece of 45" (114.3 cm) ribbon halfway through the center hole. Pull the top ribbon back down through the top hole and then back up through the center hole. Pull the bottom ribbon up through the bottom hole and bring it to the center hole to tie it in a bow. Trim the ends as desired.

3 Cut seven pieces of 12" (30.5 cm) square card stock into 6" (15.2 cm) squares for journaling. Tuck a couple of squares into each pocket and put the rest into the large vellum envelope on the inside back cover.

Studio Tip

Journaling may not be everyone's cup of tea, even though they'd like to remember a special time. Add a tag to the large vellum envelope with journaling prompts for the new mom. Ideas include: cravings, doctor visits, nesting episodes, nursery preparations, and anticipations. This way, mom can jot down little notes or sketches without becoming overwhelmed.

Inspiration 101

Right about now you may be saying to yourself, "This baby stuff is all fine and good, but how do I get started? Where do I find *my* inspiration? Where do I get *my* color, design, and style ideas?" We'll let you in on a little secret: we get inspiration from dozens of sources every day.

Mostly, it's all around us—in the fabric on a cute skirt, in the intense color of the flowers on a beautiful plant, or in a great magazine we just found at the newsstand. One of our favorite ways to spend an afternoon is at the bookstore. Between the magazine section, the art books, and a tall iced mocha from the friendly barista at the coffee counter, we've surely died and landed in design heaven. We surround ourselves with color, texture, and design on a daily basis and we live with the art and artists we most admire.

It seems like almost everyone we draw inspiration from has written a book, been published in a magazine, or has a website; and it's easy to refer to these for a quick idea when you're stumped or having trouble getting started with an art project. But poring over a bound manuscript when you have some time and really drinking it in is the best way we've found to feed the artistic soul.

So once you've purchased your book or magazine (or both), it's time to get to know them. We recommend a comfortable chair—on the beach, under a shady tree, or on the porch—and a journal for taking notes, jotting ideas, and sketching out things you'd like to try. Who do we admire? So glad you asked! We love to tell people about the artists we like. Here's a short list to get you started:

Carolyn Quartermaine—Her luscious, rich, and scrumptious interiors encourage us to incorporate French ephemera and silk ribbons, juxtaposed with metallic script, in our work. You may say that our nod to a sophisticated baby can be traced right back to Carolyn's inspiring work.

Jill Schwartz—This funky artist blends vintage details with the most glorious array of papers. Choose a trio of patterns and textures and start to lay them out with your project in mind. Metal findings complete the look, whether added to corners or making a cameo appearance front and center. The Mixed Mediums have been known to work with Jill's style in mind on everything from file folders to picture frames.

Brian Andreas—Author, poet, artist, and truth teller, Brian lights a fire within us to make art with meaning and heart—to tell a story through pictures and words. His stick-style drawings and bursts of color are perfect for motivating artwork for a child's room. Whimsical text is a trademark element of his style.

Anna Corba—A true kindred spirit, we love Anna's way with paper and ephemera. She teaches us that anything can be dressed up with vintage text, or a little ribbon with a skeleton key hanging from it. Everything looks better with a tag or an antiqued label!

Sarah Lugg—Her nickname is the "Tag Lady" and no one has inspired us more with her tag collages than Sarah. When we see little white buttons, we think Sarah. When we see tiny shells formed into a heart, we think Sarah. When you see us make paper cone party hats, you can thank Sarah.

Tracy Porter—The way this artist/designer turns the ordinary into art persuades us to look at all things for baby with new eyes. What might have been just an ordinary chandelier providing light in a nursery becomes a unique piece of family history with ancestors watching over the newest member of the tribe.

Rachel Ashwell—This queen of shabby chic reminds us to soften our edges, distress our papers, and crackle our painted canvases and cards. While she might be a principal in the home décor market, we can't help but be inspired by her way with soft color, use of vintage prints, and love for all things tarnished and old.

Favorite Magazines for Inspiration

Better Homes and Gardens specialty publications

Cloth Paper Scissors

Country Living

Domino

La Vie Claire

Legacy

Martha Stewart Living

Mary Engelbreit's Home Companion

Quilting Arts magazine

Somerset Studio

Veranda

Victoria (no longer in print—look for old copies at thrift stores or online)

Leftovers
Quick Ideas for Using Your Scraps

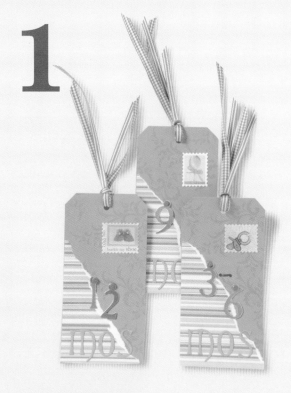

Sizing Baby Up:
Hanger Labels

Keeping baby's new wardrobe organized according to size can be a struggle! Use these brightly colored tags to divide three- to six-month garments from nine- or twelve-month sizes.

① Cut tags out of orange card stock. Stamp a leaf pattern onto the tag with a watermark ink pad.

② Tear decorative paper to fit the tag. Use die-cut letters and metal numbers to differentiate each clothing size. Embellish with a baby-themed sticker.

③ Thread coordinating ribbons through the hole in the tag. Tie to a child-sized hanger for a thoughtful gift!

Bring It Back:
Bookplates for Baby

Bookplates are perfect for a new library. As the little one's book collection grows, so does the need to keep track of his favorite volumes. These toile tags come together in a snap and are sitting pretty in their own library pocket.

① Cut tags out of toile paper.

② Computer generate *This Little Book Belongs to* and the baby's name, sans first initial. Print onto white paper and sponge with blue ink. Stamp a leaf pattern with blue ink onto a library pocket. Glue titles onto the tags and library pocket.

③ Add a die-cut letter to the beginning of the name. Thread coordinating ribbon through the hole in the tag.

3

Studio Tip

Keep those leftover rub-on letters in a variety of fonts for a ransom-style note, or make a series of monogrammed cards with the differing styles.

A Is for Abby: Monogrammed Note Cards

Before you put your paints and brushes away, coat a few square cards with extra paint and crackle medium. You'll be glad you did! Making baby his or her own monogrammed note cards is the perfect way to send a quick thank-you note for the unexpected baby blanket and package of onesies.

① Paint square cards with acrylic paint. When dry, paint a coat of crackling medium on top. When the medium is tacky, paint with a contrasting color, allowing the paint to crack and separate.

② When the cards are dry, add leftover rub-on letters and a monogram in the bottom-right corners.

③ Tie each card with two-sided satin ribbon. You can add a print of baby's foot on the back to personalize each card, too!

The first eight months of a pregnancy pass by quickly with the building anticipation, but the last few weeks can drag on while the parents-to-be anxiously await the newest family member. The nest is ready and the bag is packed. Thankfully, the nesting phase has set in and the house has never been cleaner. Take pictures, it might not be this way for long! When baby arrives, the universe shifts.

People who say they sleep like a baby usually don't have one.

—LEO J. BURKE

This chapter offers ideas to commemorate this exciting time. Posh paper announcements grace the pages with ideas for creative ways of personalizing the good news. Clever frames made from individual coin holders can travel with you everywhere, and fine art–inspired brag books give proud parents boasting rights. Mom and Grandma will be happy to show off little darlings on the Photo Memory Bracelet with sparkling crystals.

And, although baby books are a familiar tradition, the Customized Keepsake Suitcase offers a delightful way to easily save the precious three-dimensional items such as the hospital bracelet, the first tiny cap, and even a DVD of the birth or baby's first few days. The Big Boy Baby Book is another stylish memory-keeper for saving other treasures.

The projects in On-Time Arrival help to celebrate this wonderful time because having a baby doesn't mean the time to create has ended—it only means that naps are precious and the memories created and saved are even more so.

Accessories and Announcements

Babies do not travel lightly: Call it gear, accoutrement, or just plain stuff. Whether you are off to a playdate or to see relatives in another state, parents are baggage handlers…and stroller pushers…and car seat adjusters. We don't have a solution for all the schlepping that goes with parenthood, but we do offer an artistic solution for identifying baby's belongings.

Somewhere between an ID and a business card, personalized information tags may be the versatile accessory to announce a child's arrival date or help you spot baby's gear when it arrives on the airport baggage carousel. If you want to make one for yourself, try a matching tag to show off your fashionable new diaper bag.

Take your color schemes and designs from the nursery décor or your favorite children's books. Baby stores are also a source for the latest themes and designs that can be easily adapted to your custom set of baby tags. When laminated or placed in a purchased tag holder, they will meet your needs for the wear and tear that comes with lugging duffels, backpacks and roll-ons for toddlers.

MATERIALS

- purchased luggage tag holders (leather, plastic, Lucite)
- acetate transparencies
- decorative papers
- adhesive glue dots or tape
- rub-on letters or stickers
- ribbon
- embellishments
- optional: hook and loop tape (such as Velcro)

TOOLS

- basic tool kit (see page 10)
- tag template (see page 105)

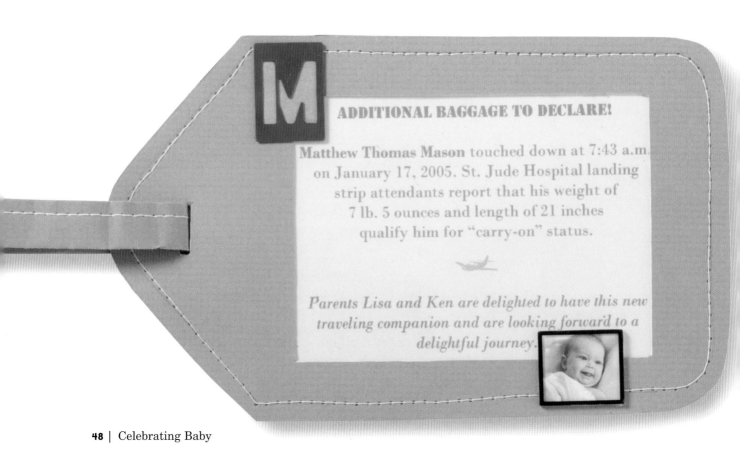

ADDITIONAL BAGGAGE TO DECLARE!

Matthew Thomas Mason touched down at 7:43 a.m. on January 17, 2005. St. Jude Hospital landing strip attendants report that his weight of 7 lb. 5 ounces and length of 21 inches qualify him for "carry-on" status.

Parents Lisa and Ken are delighted to have this new traveling companion and are looking forward to a delightful journey.

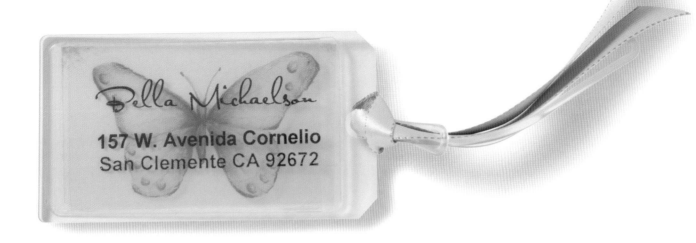

Bella Michaelson
157 W. Avenida Cornelio
San Clemente CA 92672

Making the Airport Announcement

INSTRUCTIONS

The luggage tag theme for this birth announcement could be reworded and used as a shower invitation. Carry out the airport theme at the shower by placing the gifts in open suitcases.

1. Resize the tag template (see page 105) on a copy machine if you prefer a smaller or larger version.

2. If the paper you are using will go through a copy machine, make two copies of the template for each invitation.

3. Cut a window out of one side of the template. Cut the slot for the strap out of both sides.

4. Design the announcement information and size to fit the window. Computer generate and print.

5. Assemble the back of the tag, announcement information, transparency, and front of the tag. Adhere the layers together and machine stitch ¼" (6 mm) from the edges.

6. Trace the template for the strap on matching paper. Fold over, stitch, and slip through the slot. Use hook and loop tape to secure one end to the other. You may substitute for the paper strap.

Making the Ciao Bella Announcement

INSTRUCTIONS

1. Print pertinent information on an acetate transparency and place on top of an image from a purchased transparency.

2. Insert in the pocket on the back of the Lucite tag.

Shopping Tip

If you have many announcements or invitations to make, get your family or friends together and make them assembly-line style. (They will appreciate the opportunity to learn how to do it!) You will soon be considering these tags for other purposes: thank-you cards, tree decorations, teacher gifts, door tags, golf bag tags, and scrapbook tie-ons. Give children materials and let them surprise you with their creative spin on these fun but functional tags.

VARIATIONS ON A THEME

The Prepster

This version starts with an inexpensive leather tag. Use two coats of acrylic paint to cover the front and back, then add contrasting polka dots. Print or stamp the child's name on a clear acetate transparency or piece of clear plastic. Place on top of decorative paper and center it in the tag opening. The name, address, and contact information for the parents can be printed on the back.

Circles and Squares

A faux leather tag found at a craft store combined with polka-dot paper and geometric ribbon makes a colorful fashion statement. We removed the buckle from the existing strap and attached it to ribbon for a custom look.

Ten-Minute Tags

You will appreciate the simplicity and versatility of these purchased plastic tags found at office supply stores. All you do is cut decorative paper to size, add the child's name, and attach to the adhesive backing inside. Accent the plastic straps with lively ribbons to match the paper. These are easy and inexpensive enough to use as birthday party invitations, favors, thank-you cards, or gift tags. We bet any mom would appreciate a set of six for her newborn.

Spots before Your Eyes

Use the template on page 105 for this version. Center a computer-generated name tag behind the window and adhere the front and back together with double-sided tape. Before cutting the slot and adding a ribbon, make multiple copies to tag books, toys, and other baby gear.

Paint Can Announcement

A new addition has just been completed—and we're not talking square footage. Or are we? Using a pint-sized paint can, we've played upon the home improvement fever sweeping the country.

The practical side of announcing the new baby's birth gets sassier with the accessories you add to this project. Sawdust, a bit of hardware, and paint chips wrapped up in a pretty blue paint can that can be sent through the mail make this an announcement even Bob Vila would be proud to send.

You'll find the shipping label in our Clip Art section on page 116. Tailor it with your own company name and you're ready to start your own line of custom paint cans.

Decorative blueprint paper is fairly easy to find at scrapbooking stores, but if you can't get your hands on some, look for the real thing online, from an architect in your area, in thrift stores, or perhaps from neighbors undergoing their own home improvement project.

INSTRUCTIONS

1 Spray a small paint can with metal spray paint in a well-ventilated area.

2 Photocopy the label (see page 116) and customize with your family's name, or create your own address labels using a computer. Write in your shipping addresses. Glue the label to the outside of the paint can. Glue a thin ribbon around the top of the can. Add postage-themed baby stickers to the top of the lid if desired.

3 Computer generate an announcement using the themed text: *Ground Breaking* for baby's birth date, *Square Footage and Weight* for baby's statistics, *Construction Coordinator and Day Laborer* for parents' names, and *Previously Completed Construction Projects* for the sibling's names.

4 Print the announcement and layer it to a coordinating piece of card stock and then to a piece of blueprint decorative paper using foam tape. Add brads to the corners.

5 Stamp *specimen* onto a coin envelope. Write in baby's initials and birth date. Glue ribbon around the base. Fill the envelope with plastic tool charms and hardware pieces.

6 Fill the can with a little sawdust and insert the invitation, coin envelope, and some paint chips.

MATERIALS

- pint-sized paint can (brand-new)
- spray paint
- label (see page 116)
- ribbon
- computer-generated announcement
- coin envelope
- stickers
- charms
- brads
- paint chips
- hardware
- sawdust
- card stock
- decorative paper or old blueprints
- decoupage medium
- foam tape

TOOLS

- basic tool kit (see page 10)
- rubber stamp
- ink pad

Studio Tip

The lids of these paint cans will stay on when closed and pressed firmly, making them an ideal shipping carton. Visit your post office for postage rates and information. The can's shape and size may require additional handling costs.

A CHARMED LIFE

Photo Memory Bracelet

**A simple beaded bracelet is transformed into sparkling memory jewelry with
the addition of baby photos set behind flat-backed crystals. Like badges of
honor, the crystals dangle between antique buttons, glass beads, and silver
spacers. Using an updated version of decoupage, the miniature photos are
printed on a laser printer or copier, perfectly punched out with a circle
punch, and cleverly adhered to the crystal circles. Photos can portray multiple images of a first baby, a set of siblings, an entire family, or even a collection of grandchildren.**

Making the Crystal Charms

INSTRUCTIONS

1 Reduce your photos to fit the crystals using a photocopier or laser printer
so that the photos don't bleed. On this bracelet, two different sized flat
crystals were used. Measure the flat part of the crystal to determine the
size of the photo.

2 With the circle punch upside down so that you can see the image through
the hole, crop and punch the photos.

3 Dip your finger into the soft gel and tap a small amount of the gel on the
back of the crystal to create a smooth coating. Set the crystal gel-side down
onto the front of the punched photo. The photo should stick immediately.
With the rest of the soft gel on your finger, lightly coat the back side of the
paper to give it a finish coat of gel. The gel will dry glossy.

MATERIALS

- five (or more) flat crystal beads with predrilled holes (we used beads with $1/2$" [1.3 cm] and $3/4$" [1.9 cm] diameters)
- jump rings
- beading wire
- two crimp beads
- assortment of silver decorative spacer beads
- assortment of beads (round and crystal)
- five shank-style buttons
- toggle clasp
- small black-and-white photocopied or laser-printed photos
- soft gel (gloss)

TOOLS

- basic tool kit (see page 10)
- needle-nose pliers
- towel
- needle tool or awl
- circle punch

Bead the Bracelet

INSTRUCTIONS

1 Lay a towel on the work surface to keep the beads from rolling. Most bracelets measure between $7 1/2$" and 8" (19.1 cm and 20.3 cm) long. Lay out the beads and buttons in your chosen pattern. In this bracelet, silver decorative spacers, two colors of crystal beads, small hematite beads, and antique shank buttons are strung onto the beading wire. A silver toggle clasp completes the design.

2 To begin the bracelet, cut a piece of beading wire about $1 1/2$ times longer than the finished length. Thread the end of the wire through one crimp bead, then through one side of the toggle clasp, and then back through the crimp bead. With the crimp bead snug against the toggle clasp, squeeze the crimp bead with the pliers to secure.

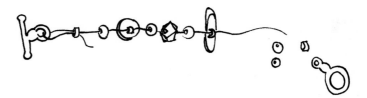

3 Thread the beads onto the wire in the desired order. To finish the beading, thread the wire through a crimp bead, through the other side of the toggle clasp, and back through the crimp bead. Secure the crimp bead, trim the remaining beading wire, and tuck the ends of the wire under the beads to hide them.

Putting It All Together

INSTRUCTIONS

1 Once the photo crystals are dry, use a needle or awl to poke a hole through the backing paper on each one.

2 Open a jump ring with the pliers and insert it into the hole of the crystal. Slip the crystals over the beaded wire and onto the bracelet. Use the pliers to close the jump ring. Repeat for each crystal, spacing them out around the bracelet.

PROUD DADDY GEAR

Travel Frame

Keep Dad in the picture with this handsome frame for on the go. Creative use of paper, snaps, and collectible coin holders makes this little project a cinch—or should we say snap? Who knew that crumpled paper could make such a great faux leather look? We did! And for fun, we packaged it in Ultrasuede to keep dad's treasure safe during travel.

INSTRUCTIONS

1 Cut two pieces of card stock 2 1/2" × 5" (6.4 × 12.7 cm) and one 1/2" × 5" (1.3 × 12.7 cm). Crumple the papers into balls, open up, and crumple again in a different direction.

2 Slightly flatten the pieces of paper and run a coordinating ink pad over them to create a leatherlike effect on the paper.

3 Mist slightly with water to help the ink soak in and spread. Iron with a craft iron on a craft sheet to completely smooth out the card stock.

4 Add half of a snap to the front of one of the bigger pieces of paper. With the inked side faceup, place it 3/4" (1.9 cm) from the right side (short side) and 1 1/4" (3.2 cm) from the top (long side).

MATERIALS

- card stock (preferably textured)
- cardboard collectible coin holders
- decorative papers
- snaps
- ink
- glue stick

TOOLS

- basic tool kit (see page 10)
- silicone craft sheet
- snap setter
- craft iron
- water mister bottle

5 Place the two larger pieces of card stock back to back with the uninked sides touching. These will make the cover. Cut $1/2$" (1.3 cm) strips of decorative paper and fold them in half lengthwise. Adhere the cover pieces together by gluing these strips around the perimeter.

6 Fold the small inked strip in half with the ink side showing. Open this back up and add the other snap half to the inked side, $1/2$" (1.3 cm) from the fold line. Glue the uninked sides and fold together to create the strap.

7 With the inside of the cover faceup (the snap on the cover should be face-down on the left side), glue the strap to the right-hand side of the cover by centering it between the top and bottom edges of the cover and leaving $1^1/2$" (3.8 cm) off the right-hand side with the snap on the strap faceup.

8 Cut two $1^1/4$" (3.2 cm) squares of decorative paper and glue onto the inside cover leaving a $1/8$" (3 mm) border around the top, bottom, and outside edge.

9 Ink, paint, or stamp the white side of the two coin holders as desired, making sure to keep the acetate window clean.

9 Cut $5/16$" (8 mm)-wide strips of decorative paper. With the coin holder open fully, use these strips to cover the right and left short sides of the holder in the same manner as the cover was made in step 5.

10 Fold the coin holder in half and wrap the paper around the other three sides to create a pocket. With the open end at the top, glue the holder centered over one of the decorative squares inside the cover. Repeat steps 9 through 11 with the other holder.

11 Snap closed.

Studio Tip

If you just can't leave well enough alone, then cover it in faux suede! Make the optional suede cover by folding a 6" x 3$1/2$" (15.2 x 8.9 cm) piece of faux suede in half, sewing along the 3$1/2$" (9 cm) sides to create a pocket. Cut along the open side with pinking shears to finish the look. Press with a warm iron if necessary. For a traveling mom, try adding a pretty iron-on monogram.

Brag Books

We aren't sure what the national average is for the number of photos taken in baby's first year, but we are pretty sure it's close to a gazillion, plus or minus the standard deviation, of course. So we're willing to bet that these brag books just might come in handy. They aren't just cute—they are quick, too. The mat board can be cut with one spin of a rotary cutter and the inside pages get an easy torn edge. If choosing a clever binding is half the fun, you can bet that creating your cover is the other half!

INSTRUCTIONS

1 Cut two pieces of mat board $4^{3}/_{4}$" × 5" (12.1 × 12.7 cm).

2 Use a glue stick to cover both sides of each board.

3 Decorate the cover with additional pieces of card stock and embellishments.

4 Cut strips of card stock $4^{1}/_{2}$" × 9 1/2" (11.4 × 24.1 cm)

5 Tear the strips in half using a metal ruler to create two $4^{1}/_{2}$" × $4^{3}/_{4}$" (11.4 × 12.1 cm) pages.

6 Repeat step 5 until you have created the desired number of pages.

7 Line up the front and back cover with all the pages inside. All covers and pages should be flush against the spine side (the torn edges will be the outside edge, opposite the spine). Use binder clips or an oversized rubber band to secure.

8 Use the anywhere punch to punch two evenly spaced $^{1}/_{4}$" (6 mm) holes on the spine side of the book (approximately $^{3}/_{8}$" [1 cm] from the left side, 1" [2.5 cm] from the top, and 1" [2.5 cm] from the bottom).

9 Insert a binding material of binder rings, ball chain, ribbon, or torn fabric.

10 Use customized photo corners to add photos (see Leftovers on pages 72–73) to your book or adhere a small glassine envelope filled with photo corners to the inside back cover.

MATERIALS
- mat board
- card stock
- decorative paper
- metal frame
- ribbon
- rickrack
- foam tape
- glue stick
- photo corners
- binding material

TOOLS
- basic tool kit (see page 10)
- binder clips or oversized rubber band
- anywhere punch

Studio Tip

We used black core mat board for this project but you can substitute any mat board and run a marker over the edge to get a customized color border on your covers.

VARIATIONS ON A THEME

Matisse

Intricate paper cutting is attributed to Matisse. Simple shapes color blocked on bright card stock beckon "open me." Cut your shapes freehand as Matisse did or cheat just a little with the templates on page 106.

Beach Bum

Baby blue is tweaked along with the stereotypical baby themes on this hip book. Surf, sand, and summer are held together with binder rings and say "Hang Ten Dude!" in a way all their own. Righteous.

Ride 'Em Cowpoke

Mosey to your workspace with some denim paper and a few nail heads to make this dungaree-inspired book. An old bandana serves as unique ribbon and a pocket embellishment (see template on page 107).

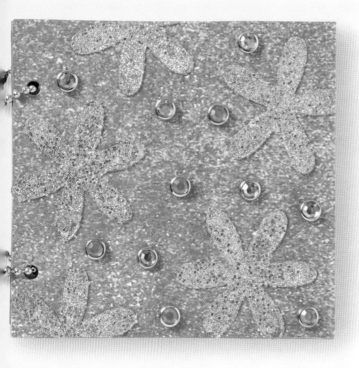

Rock Diva

All that glitters is gaudy and perfect, or so says the littlest diva. Rhinestone brads embed the cover with glitter-covered flowers. Ball chain gives this book edginess with rock-star flair.

MATERIALS

- purchased cardboard suitcase (approximately 10" × 12" [25.4 × 30.5 cm])
- decorative paper
- card stock
- vellum
- mat board strips 1¹⁄₂" (3.8 cm) wide
- small gift boxes or papier-mâché boxes
- tin (or an empty mint tin)
- ribbon
- eyelets
- round, metal-rimmed stationery tags with jump rings
- paint
- glue stick
- bookbinder's cloth or gaffer's tape

TOOLS

- basic tool kit (see page 10)
- decorative-edge scissors

MEMORY VALISE

Customized Keepsake Suitcase

Time passes so quickly when baby finally arrives! This little case holds all of those special treasures that might get lost without a special keeping place like this. The DVD holder carries precious footage of baby's first days, first bath, first yawn, and all the other wonderful things that Dad has videotaped for the proud grandparents to watch. A corseted piece of vellum hugs a stack of cards sent from well-wishers. Tiny boxes hold the first pacifier, rattle, and baby booties. A little tin offers a safe place for the hospital bracelet. Jenn received a purchased box like this when her first daughter was born. Daughter number two liked it and wanted one, too. This project was the result. (The only problem now is that big sis likes this one better!)

Making the Case Cover

INSTRUCTIONS

1 On the back side of a large piece of decorative paper trace the shape of the outside of the suitcase and cut out, allowing for seams. It may be necessary to do this in two pieces, depending on the size of your paper.

2 If necessary, use paints or permanent markers to embellish the hinged sections of the case.

3 Adhere the decorative paper to the case with a glue stick. Reinforce the adhesion by burnishing the paper with a bone folder.

4 Trace or measure the inside sides, top, and bottom. Cover the inside with decorative paper in the same fashion.

Making the Tray and Supports

INSTRUCTIONS

❶ Cut the base for the inner tray from a piece of mat board cut to the exact length and width of the inside of the case.

❷ Cut four side pieces for the tray from the mat board strips, two that measure the length of the base and two that measure the width of the base.

❸ Use bookbinder's tape or gaffer's tape to adhere the base and the sides of the tray together, and then cover with decorative paper cut to size.

❹ To create the supports, cut two more strips of mat board, one the length of the tray and one the width of the tray. Cover these with decorative paper and glue to the back and sides of the case to hold the tray in place.

Making the Boxes and Vellum Wrap

INSTRUCTIONS

❶ Use the bottom of small gift boxes or small papier-mâché boxes to hold little treasures within the case. Use a combination of paint and decorative paper to cover and decorate the boxes. Tie the boxes closed and label with small metal-rimmed tags. Customize your selection of boxes to fit your keepsake needs.

❷ To create the vellum corset wrap, cut a piece of vellum approximately 5" × 12" (12.7 × 30.5 cm). Fold back 3/4" (1.9 cm) along both of the short sides and embellish with small strips of paper cut with decorative-edge scissors. Punch holes and add eyelets. Fold the wrap around the keepsakes and lace ribbon through the eyelets.

Studio Tip
Customized Cases

We all know what can happen when overexcited fathers and new video recorders mix! And all those hundreds of hours of baby on film deserve a pretty storage place. Save the plastic DVD cases that come with sample software in the mail or buy empty cases and decorate them. Make a series of cases: Baby's First Bath, Baby's First Holiday, and Baby's First Birthday. Decorate a dozen cases and give a holiday greeting from baby by video this year.

To create the personalized DVD case inserts, you'll need decorative paper, card stock, and decorative-edge scissors. Measure the DVD case to create a template. Cut decorative paper to size using the template. Add fun labels or card stock to create a title box. Use decorative-edge scissors to add a whimsical yet classic feel to the cover. To insert the cover under the clear plastic on the DVD case, open the case until the clear plastic buckles away from the case and slip the cover in between.

RECORD

1925

PHOTOS

SNAPSHOTS

2005

RECORD

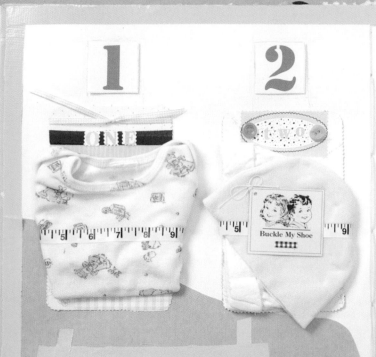

1 2 3 4

ONE

two

THREE

four

Buckle My Shoe

Buckle My Shoe

ONE TWO
BUCKLE MY SHOE

THREE FOUR
CLOSE THE DOOR

MATERIALS

- large-format book (teacher's supply store)
- foam board (such as Fome-Cor)
- decorative papers
- poster board
- card stock
- buttons
- batting
- chenille fabric
- rickrack
- ephemera
- family photos
- colored duct tape
- ruler tape
- metal clips
- plastic paper clips
- rub-on titles
- acetate transparencies
- jewel case
- adhesive-backed CD envelopes
- colored portfolios
- newborn clothing items
- cotton cloth
- waxed thread
- spray adhesive
- E6000 glue
- adhesive dots
- double-sided tape
- white gesso
- indelible marker
- crayons
- quilt basting spray (optional)

TOOLS

- basic tool kit (see page 10)
- paintbrush
- sewing machine

BIG BOY BABY BOOK

A Grand Tribute to Baby

When we envision projects for babies, we often think small—itsy-bitsy, teeny-weenie, and precious. This large-format baby book takes a different approach—call it hunky-chunky, and rough-and-ready.

A quilted paper patchwork cover (yes, it is actually quilted on the sewing machine) tells you this is for a baby, but when opened up, this book is anything *but* precious. Though it looks time consuming, this album comes together quickly by using a purchased book as the base. Add a paper-quilted cover, then embellish the interior pages with altered office supplies. Pages are edged in duct tape, and basic office supplies—including portfolios, CD holders, and envelopes—are attached to hold copies of birth records, medical information, and memorabilia. These generic items are painted and embellished to invite a peek inside.

The numbers pages are soft and sentimental with groupings of baby items on numerical flash cards. But the duct tape and bold stenciled letters remind you this is a Big Boy Baby Book.

Making the Book

1 Cut two pieces of foam board to fit the front and back covers of a purchased book. Adhere with spray adhesive to the covers.

2 Cover the inside pages with your choice of material: poster board, Fun Foam (found at craft stores), felt, fabric, or paper.

3 Adhere colored duct tape to the edges of each page.

4 Wrap the spine area with chenille fabric and adhere with adhesive dots.

Making the Quilt Cover (see page 68)

1 Measure the cover to determine the number and size of squares you want. Cut the desired number of squares from decorative paper in coordinating colors and patterns.

2 Cut a piece of batting approximately the size of the cover (it can be trimmed after sewing). Apply a coat of quilt basting spray to the top surface of the batting.

3 Starting from the left side, place a row of paper squares on top of the batting and machine sew in place vertically on the right-hand side of the squares. Repeat with the next row (center), stitching on the right-hand side of the squares and placing each square as close as possible to the first row.

Repeat with the last row, placing the squares close to the adjacent line of squares.

4 Machine stitch a horizontal line between each row of squares after the vertical rows are in place.

5 Using waxed thread, tie buttons to the inside corners of each square.

6 Affix the paper quilt to a backing of heavy paper with spray adhesive.

7 Affix large rickrack around the entire quilt using adhesive dots.

8 Using waxed thread, tie large buttons to each outside corner of the quilt. Affix the quilt to the cover of the book after the inside pages are finished using adhesive dots or double-sided tape.

Making the Portfolio Spread (left-hand side)

1 Cover the flap of a purchased portfolio with decorative paper. Using a dry brush, apply white gesso to the flap and front of the portfolio. Write a date on a purchased plastic paper clip with an indelible marker and place on the portfolio flap.

2 Place a photograph of a baby under an acetate transparency trimmed to the same size. Place a copy of a family photograph in a plastic jewel case. Embellish the photograph and jewel case with rub-on titles.

3 Affix all items with adhesive dots or double-sided tape. Decorative paper or ephemera can be added to the pages before other items are affixed.

Making the Portfolio Spread (right-hand side)

1 Affix two strips of varying widths of decorative paper to the portfolio flap. Using a dry brush, apply white gesso to the flap and front of the portfolio. Embellish with rub-on titles.

2 Insert matching decorative paper into the flaps of two plastic, adhesive-backed jewel cases. Cut paper to fit the curve of the flap. Insert printed ephemera into the jewel case. Embellish with colorful buttons and ruler tape. Affix all items with adhesive dots or double-sided tape.

Making the Numbers Page

1 Cover pages with white poster board trimmed to size.

❷ Cut a curvilinear pocket for the bottom of the page and affix it with colored duct tape.

❸ Computer generate *one-two buckle my shoe* in a stencil font and print on decorative paper. Cut out and affix to the front of the pocket with duct tape.

❹ Computer generate the numbers in a stencil font and print on card stock. Cut out the numbers into squares and adhere across the top of the pages. Use a crayon to make a border around each number. The cards behind the baby items are made to look like numerical flash cards.

❺ Cover four cards measuring approximately 4 1/2" × 7 1/2" (11.4 × 19.1 cm) with decorative papers and embellishments.

❻ Computer generate the numbers and cut out. Glue each number to the top of each card.

❼ Attach one baby item to card one, two items on card two, and so on, using the appropriate type of glue or attachment device for each item.

Making the Lattice Page

❶ To make a memo board inside the book, tear strips of cotton cloth to approximately 1" (2.5 cm) wide and 14" (35.6 cm) long. (This measurement will depend on the size of the page.)

❷ Create a lattice on top of a page covered with felt by weaving the strips over and under one another.

❸ When the lattice is completely laid out, remove one strip at and time and apply quilt basting spray to the back side of the fabric.

❹ Replace the strip and proceed in this way, spraying and replacing one strip at a time. Secure the intersections with a few stitches through the backing page. Add a button for more decoration.

Painting Baby Steps

Paper addicts are constantly tempted by papers available in specialty, craft, and scrapbook stores. Even with this huge selection now available, we sometimes find a paper that is close to what we want but not just the right shade or texture. Consider this a positive situation…an excuse to get messy and start mixing mediums!

Your next stop is the paint aisle. After perusing the art supply store, take some time to see what the home improvement stores offer in glazes, tools for faux painting techniques, and stencils. These stores also offer paint in spray cans that will give you unusual effects such as hammered metal, sand, or suede.

Read on and discover how to customize your paper with new paint techniques and materials such as cheesecloth, kosher salt, and dish soap. Be brave, get messy, and experiment.

Gesso

Traditionally used to prepare a canvas for painting, gesso comes in both black and white. Add any acrylic paint to white gesso to create a custom color. This makes a good undercoat when you are applying multiple layers of paint. White gesso is never far from our worktable. We use a dry paintbrush to apply it over the surface to create a unified look on collages (**a**). For the popular shabby-chic look, apply a coat of gesso or white paint, then wipe it off with a paper towel to alter the color and texture of the surface, as we did in the Big Boy Baby Book (page 67).

Spray Paint

Spraying a light mist of black matte spray paint over colored paper results in an interesting texture (**b**). For sparkle and shine, splatter silver and gold metallic spray paint in a light mist, as in the Totes, Bibs, and Placemats (page 77).

Glaze

A thin glaze of blue is painted over a white or light color base and then pressed into with cheesecloth to make fun faux denim on a Hanging Paper Frame Variation (page 27) (**c**). With an inexpensive brush and some pages salvaged from a vintage book, we created a whole new paper that we used to embellish the Repurposed Mobile (page 15).

Watercolor and Ink

Cover a thick piece of watercolor paper with splashes of water to prepare you paper surface to accept a wash of color. Next, pick up some color with a very wet brush and touch it to the wet surface of the paper so the color spreads (**d**). Add more water with or without color to continue filling the color wash. After the paper is dry, use it as the base of a collage or trace a template onto it like we did in our birthday hat project (page 80). Throw salt on wet watercolored paper and let it dry. Use a small amount for a light mottled look (**e**) or up your salt intake for a crazy textured look.

We used walnut ink to age a too-sweet pink paper used on our Heritage Chandelier project (page 95). By diluting the ink with water and applying it in layers, the depth of color can be controlled (**f**).

Acrylic Paint

Standard artist acrylics come in tubes and are opaque. Fluid acrylics are transparent and can be used to tint gesso, glazes, or gels. To get the marblelike texture, add equal parts acrylic, dish soap, and water to the bottom of the plastic cup and insert a straw. Blow through the straw until the cup fills up with colored bubbles. By placing a canvas board up against the cup (**g**), we were able to transfer the bubbles onto the canvas to create the texture on our Climbing Jacob's Ladder Growth Chart and Memo Board (page 91).

Simple items, such as the bottom of a paint bottle or number stamps, can be dipped into acrylic inks and stamped onto a project as ink (**h**).

Gel

Soft gel in matte, gloss, or semigloss can be used as an effective medium for decoupage. Soft gel was used to seamlessly cover the Repurposed Mobile (page 15) in a thick handmade paper (**i**). Tinting the gel with fluid acrylics adds a soft glow to a project. If you need to attach buttons or other three-dimensional items, gel can be used as a great flexible glue for this as well.

Experiment and explore with paint, gels, inks, and glazes! The process of taking a purchased paper and making it your own will always keep your artwork looking unique and original.

Leftovers
Quick Ideas for Using Your Scraps

You won't need to scale down your expectations with these petite accessories.

1

Hanging around Town

Hang it from your purse, the diaper bag or your rearview mirror. Scraps make this a quick project from start to finish.

1 Cover the front half of a coin holder (with the plastic removed) with card stock.

2 Place the covered coin holder over a photo, adhere, and trim the edges.

3 Cover the back of the photo with card stock, punch a hole, and add ball chain and ribbon.

Feeling Cornered?

Small strips of paper and scraps of rub-ons turn into fun photo corners. Use these in a brag book (page 58) or give a set as a gift in a small glassine envelope.

1 Cut strips between ¹/₄" (6 mm) and ¹/₂" (1.3 cm) wide and 2" (5.1 cm) and 3" (7.6 cm) long.

2 In the middle of the strip, fold back each side at a 45 degree angle to create a corner.

3 Use decorative-edge scissors to trim off the excess strip, decorate with rub-ons, and add a piece of double-sided tape with removable backing.

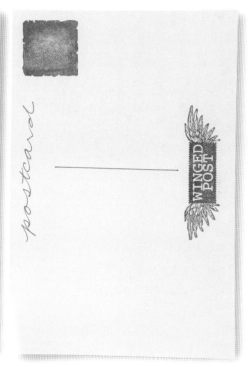

Wish You Were Here

These photo postcards are a great way to use up extra pictures and to keep in touch at the same time. They are the perfect things to send, when you care enough to send the very cutest.

1 Glue a photo to card stock and trim around the edges

2 Add *Postcard* to the top center of the card stock and a center dividing line.

THE SURVIVAL GUIDE

it's all relative

LITTLE BEAR'S ETIQUETTE BOOK

This chapter focuses on art and creativity to celebrate the milestones of baby's first year. Inspiration and information for the projects came from the many hours the Mixed Mediums spent in baby stores examining everything from clothing tags to logos, and diaper bags to T-shirts.

Humans are the only animals that have children on purpose with the exception of guppies, who like to eat theirs.

—P. J. O'ROURKE

In our quest to translate what we saw into projects for the books we used paper and mixed-media art techniques to reflect the humor, historical references, color, and designs we observed in the lively and ever-changing baby industry. We developed tote bags to fashionably carry baby gear and colorful accessories and books that double as learning tools.

From paper party hats that have a one-day life span to a timeless crystal chandelier, you will see examples incorporating unusual items to make your projects personal and unique: a vintage yardstick in a growth chart, paint chips on a clock face, and clear plastic tubing used as a tote bag handle.

To supplement our materials stash, we foraged for old baby clothing patterns, photographs, and vintage books and found inspiration in container stores, office supply stores, and paper stores from Beverly Hills to Boston. You just never know what will drive your next new, old, funky, elegant, colorful, or contemporary masterpiece.

Totes, Bibs, and Place Mats

They say "it's all in the accessories" and that is certainly the case when it's time to include tiny diners in the restaurant reservation count or when visiting family and friends.

Transforming purchased gift bags into smart totes and purses ensures that you can leave the diaper bag behind and still carry baby's eating essentials with a bit of panache. Tucked inside, decorative paper place mats provide a sanitary eating surface and are convenient and portable for on-the-go parents.

The clear adhesive coating is easy to clean and they roll up and slide into a tube for easy transporting. Colorful patterns on the place mats are fun and educational and help entertain the child during everyday dining as well.

Portable, disposable bibs to match the totes are fast and easy to make out of clothlike paper tablecloths found at warehouse stores. We stamped and decorated the bibs and then covered the surface with clear contact paper. In the process, we discovered that making six was almost as easy as making one when we did them assembly-line style.

Finish off the dining set with disposable plastic baby spoons and forks and a book or small toy to keep baby amused while learning the art of fine dining.

Making the Black-and-White Tote Bag

1 Carefully open up all the glued seams in a purchased gift bag.

2 Lay flat and cover each section separately (front, back, and sides) with checkered adhesive backed contact paper.

3 Allow an extra 2" (5.1 cm) of contact paper to fold over at the top, then trim sides if needed.

4 Create a decorative paper panel with various fonts and letters, and attach it to the front of the tote with spray adhesive.

5 For the handle, fill a 13" (33 cm) length of clear plastic tubing with small beads. Insert a larger bead at each end to secure the smaller beads inside.

6 Make a hole slightly larger than the circumference of the tubing on the sides of the tote. Insert the tubing from the outside and secure to the inside with double-sided adhesive.

7 Tie a ribbon at the base of the handle on each side to cover the hole.

Making the Purse-Shaped Bag

1 Affix decorative paper to all outside surfaces of a purchased paper gift bag. (We used one paper for the front and back and contrasting paper on the sides.)

2 Place a layer of clear contact paper over all outside surfaces.

3 Attach a purchased Lucite handle with ribbon.

4 Affix a clear plastic pocket to the front of the purse to hold a small book, teething ring, or toy.

Making the Place Mats

1 Use the length of the plastic or cardboard tube to determine the height of the place mat so it will roll up and fit inside.

2 Cut the paper to size and decorate if desired.

3 For lighter-weight paper, affix a paper backing with adhesive or glue.

4 Cover the place mat with clear contact paper.

Making the Clear Plastic or Cardboard Tubes

❶ Cover the tube with decorative paper to match the place mats.

Making the Bibs

❶ Trace the bib template (see page 109) onto a paper table cover.

❷ Cut and decorate with stamped images.

❸ Cover the bib front with contact paper.

❹ Machine or hand stitch ribbon ties at the top.

Birthday Hats and Blowers

Mark the first birthday milestone with paper panache. Make a special one-of-a-kind hat just for baby or make one for each of the party guests. Delightfully quick to make, these party hats can be completely customized with ribbon, tissue paper, or paper-frilled trims. Boring generic blowers are pulled apart for their noisemaker and repurposed into a lovely party plaything. Thin handmade papers can easily be glued to card stock to make a sturdy base for the matching hat and blowers. The featured hat and blower (above, center) was made from quickly painted watercolor paper for a soft, shimmery look. Try adding ribbon ties for baby's hat and elastic bands for older children attending the party. For a keepsake, hang baby's hat upside down as a paper cone and fill with special mementos from his special day.

MATERIALS

- watercolor paper (card-stock weight or heavier)
- shimmery water-colors
- ink pad
- kosher or coarse salt
- tissue paper
- noisemakers removed from generic party blowers
- adhesive foam squares
- $1/4$" (6 mm)-wide industrial-strength tape
- ribbon or elastic (optional)

TOOLS

- basic tool kit (see page 10)
- paintbrush
- rubber stamp
- sewing machine
- templates (pages 107–108)

Preparing the Paper

1 Randomly paint swatches and splashes of watercolors onto the paper. Sprinkle random wet spots with salt and let dry.

2 Remove the salt from the paper.

3 Randomly stamp the paper with a butterfly stamp.

Making the Hat

1 Trace the hat template (see page 108) onto the back of the watercolor paper and cut out.

2 Place a strip of tape along one side of the hat starting about 1" (2.5 cm) below the top point. Round the hat to create a cone shape and secure along the taped edge

3 Fold a piece of tissue paper back and forth on top of itself to create a stack of strips at least 18" (45.7 cm) long and 3" (7.6 cm) wide. Machine sew the pieces together down the long center of the paper.

4 Cut approximately $1/2$" (1.3 cm) off each long side of the strips to remove the folds and then make 1" (2.5 cm) cuts every $1/4$" (6 mm), perpendicular to the stitching, to create fringe.

5 Adhere the fringe to the bottom of the hat and scrunch it to make it full and fluffy.

6 Stamp and cut out an extra butterfly and attach it to the blower with an adhesive foam square.

7 Add ribbon or elastic to keep the hat on baby's head, if desired.

Creating the Blower

1 Trace the blower template (see page 107) onto the back of the watercolor paper and cut out.

2 Place a strip of tape along one side of the blower. Round the blower and secure along the taped edge.

3 Place tape along the small end of the blower and insert into a noisemaker.

4 Create fringe (see steps 3 and 4 from Making the Hat, above) or use leftover fringe from the hat and attach it to the blower.

5 Stamp and cut out an extra butterfly and attach it to the blower with an adhesive foam square.

VARIATIONS ON A THEME

Big, juicy watermelon was the inspiration for this luscious birthday set. The thin, green handmade paper was attached to a piece of neutral card stock to make a strong decorative paper. A piece of bright red paper cut to the same curve as the bottom of the hat and scored down the middle makes this whimsical hat and blower trim.

Carry out a theme throughout a party with this fun paper. A large sheet of paper suitable for gift wrapping is cut apart into individual blocks and then glued down onto a piece of red card stock before being traced and cut out.

For the more serious, art-loving baby, this party set uses fine, handmade Italian marbled paper, velvet ribbon, sheet music, and copper metal embellishments. Don't be afraid to tone down or coordinate your metal embellishments with a little touch of permanent opaque ink.

This birthday combination is certainly not geometrically challenged. Strips of double-sided paper are attached to the blower and hat and then curled back on themselves for a lot of pomp and circumstance!

The Survival Guide | **83**

A Book about Family

As baby begins to explore his environment and surroundings, he is curious to learn more about the people in his life and their names. This book was created with that need in mind.

Using a child's board book with windows and doors, we adapted it to fit our needs and story. This book's shape and style lent itself perfectly for this purpose. The cutout opening at the top of the book makes it perfect for little hands to carry.

With a nod to children's book artist Eric Carle and his tale of *Brown Bear, Brown Bear, What Do You See?*, we've crafted our own version using pictures of baby and his family members along with text that introduces each person behind a door. Stylish ribbons tied to the cover of the book add a whimsical frill that little fingers will enjoy.

Making the Cover

1 Paint a child's board book with several coats of gesso. When dry, paint the cover of the book with acrylic paint. Let dry.

2 Trace the cover of the book onto a piece of decorative paper. Cut out and glue to the front cover. Add metal charms to the bottom corners.

3 Place a child's photo in a metal frame. Glue the frame to a piece of coordinating card stock that has been trimmed with decorative-edge scissors. Layer the frame piece to a panel of decorative paper that has been trimmed with decorative-edge scissors and glue to the front cover with a square panel of card stock.

4 Spell out *it's all relative* with die-cut letters and glue around the framed picture.

5 Tie the handle opening of the cover with coordinating ribbons.

MATERIALS

- child's board book
- decorative paper
- charms
- ribbon
- card stock
- die-cut letters
- rub-on letters
- frames
- metal clips
- oval sticker
- epoxy stickers
- photographs
- mounting foam tape
- adhesive
- gesso
- acrylic paint

TOOLS

- basic tool kit (see page 10)
- decorative-edge scissors
- paintbrushes
- permanent marker

baby baby

WHO DO YOU SEE?

I see

mommy
&
gramma

lookin

at me

Making the Inside of the Book

① Trace the book cover again onto a piece of decorative paper and cut out. Glue to the right page of the first spread of the book. Use a craft knife to cut the paper around the circle of the door. Paint the left page with acrylic paint.

② Use rub-on letters to spell out *baby baby* and *mommy & gramma looking at me.* Use die-cut letters to spell out *I see.* Add epoxy stickers to the right page.

③ Trim a piece of coordinating card stock with decorative-edge scissors and add thin strips behind the door to create a decorative border.

④ Using the same scissors, cut a scrap of coordinating paper into a rectangle. Handwrite *who do you see?* on a sticker with a permanent marker. Attach to the left page with several layers of mounting foam tape. Add two metal clips to each side of the rectangle.

⑤ Place child's photo in a metal frame and mount it to a decorative panel with mounting foam tape. Glue to the left page of the book with a card stock panel trimmed with decorative-edge scissors.

⑥ Glue a piece of ribbon across the decorative panel.

⑦ Place a picture of family members (Mommy and Gramma) behind the door so that their faces show through the circle in the door.

TEN MINUTES TO ORANGE

Paint Chip Clock

More than just a timepiece, this rainbow clock displays visual information for children in the form of circles, squares, numbers, and colors. It can set the palette for an entire room or blend in with various styles of nursery décor.

This just-in-time decorative accessory can be made for a shower gift or, if you prefer to give it after the baby is born, you can personalize the clock by adding the baby's name and date of birth to the front or back.

Another alternative for this custom clock is to make hand-painted versions of paint chips and give the colors names such as "Tonka Toy Red," "Garrett's Green," or "Baby Toes Pink."

We also see clock hands in the form of crayons, paintbrushes, and colored markers.

INSTRUCTIONS

❶ Remove the clock hands before you work on the clock.

❷ Divide the clock into quarters and mark where the hands will point at 12, 3, 6, and 9 o'clock.

❸ Lay out the paint chips in color sequence and determine how many will fit in each quadrant.

❹ Trim or overlap the paint chips to fit the space. They do not need to extend all the way to the center, but they do need to be long enough to fit under the edge of the color wheel in the center.

❺ Work around the clock, section by section, until the surface is covered with paint chips.

❻ Affix the paint chips with double-sided adhesive tape.

❼ Make a hole in the center of the color wheel and affix double-sided adhesive dots in the center of the clock.

❽ Affix number stickers at the 12, 3, 6, and 9 o'clock positions.

❾ Use small wooden blocks to indicate all other numbers.

❿ Reattach the clock hands or replace with ones of your choice.

MATERIALS

- round clock (new or used)
- paint chips in a rainbow of colors
- double-sided adhesive tape
- color wheel (diameter will depend on the size of the clock)
- small square wooden blocks
- adhesive-backed numbers
- clock hands of your choice
- adhesive dots

TOOLS

- basic tool kit (see page 10)

Growth Chart and Memo Board

MATERIALS

- card stock
- five 9" × 12" (22.9 × 30.5 cm) canvas art boards
- dish soap
- acrylic paint
- soft gel (matte)
- ribbon (two of one color measuring 60" [152.4 cm] and one of another color measuring 48" [121.9 cm]; we used white and green)
- eyelets
- ruler clip art (see page 115)

TOOLS

- basic tool kit (see page 10)
- heavy-duty hole punch
- eyelet setter
- number rubber stamps
- plastic cup
- drinking straw
- height marking tabs template (see page 107)

This project was inspired by an old Jacob's ladder, a mind-boggling toy that can easily absorb an entire lazy afternoon with its mesmerizing motion. Each section of this growth chart is painted with bubbles and then secured with ribbon creating what "grew" into a memo board as well. A vintage collapsible ruler (see page 115) was scanned for the measuring part and then decoupaged and glazed to the boards. This project could easily be reduced to make smaller wall art or reduced even smaller to make a special card. Try the bubble technique (See From the Studio, Acrylic Paint, on page 70) but be warned, you might get carried away. Make sure to protect the work surface and wear old clothing. Oh, and try not to have too much fun.

Preparing the Boards

1 Cover each of the boards with bubble paint. Let dry.
With liquid acrylics or watered-down acrylic paint, add a thin layer of color over the bubble paint to tone it down.

2 Use soft gel (matte) to glue down the ruler on the right-hand side of the boards. Lightly tint some gel with yellow acrylic and rub over the ruler to give it a slight tint.

3 Use paints and stamps to randomly stamp numbers. Use the bottom of the paint bottles as a stamp to paint "bubbles." Let dry.

Creating the Tabs

1 Trace the tab template (see page 107) onto card stock.

2 Cut and decorate with stamped numbers.

Making the Jacob's Ladder

When adding the ribbon, keep in mind that the ruler needs to go in the right order, that the ribbon is glued only to the back side, and that each board has either two ribbons or one center ribbon on it at any one time.

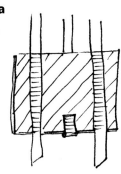

1 Starting with your bottom board facedown, glue one white ribbon down the left side 1½" (3.8 cm) from the left edge, leaving a 5" (12.7 cm) tail hanging off the bottom.

2 Repeat step 1 on the right-hand side.

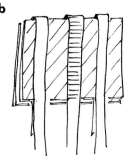

3 Slide the green ribbon under the boards so that it is lying down the middle of the board with a 5" (12.7 cm) tail hanging below the bottom and the rest is at the top of the board. Glue the green 5" (12.7 cm) tail up onto the board (**a**).

4 Flip the board over and fold down the two outside ribbons. Place the second board facedown onto the first, making sure the ruler continues in the correct order.

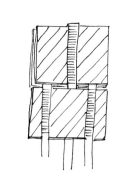

5 Fold the center ribbon over and glue down the back of the second board (**b**).

6 Fold the two outside ribbons up over the second board. Lay the third board facedown over the green ribbon below the first and second boards. Fold the two outside ribbons down onto the back of the third board and glue down, making sure to keep the ribbons taut (**c**).

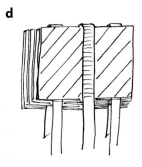

7 Flip the third board up onto the first and second boards, and fold down the green and white ribbons. Place the fourth board facedown on top of the other boards keeping the ruler in order. Fold the green ribbon over and glue down, folding up the white ribbons (**d**).

8 Place the last board below the stack and fold the white ribbons down over the last board and glue down. Fold the remaining green tail up and glue to the back of the last board (**e**).

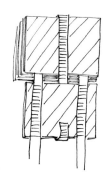

9 To hang the ladder, use the heavy-duty hole punch to punch two holes in the top of the top board and add eyelets if desired. Pull the white outside ribbon through the holes and tie into a bow. Tie the two bottom tails into a decorative knot or cut off.

Heritage Chandelier

MATERIALS

- acetate transparency
- chandelier (or sconce, lamp shade, etc)
- Canson paper
- photographs (see pages 118–119)
- embellishments for crystals
- glass paint
- foil
- foil glue
- pages from a vintage children's book (see page 111)
- Diamond Glaze
- crystals or pendants with a flat side
- thin wire or jump rings
- adhesive (glue stick or Zots)
- Flamex or other fire-retardant spray for paper (see Product Resources, page 124)

TOOLS

- basic tool kit (see page 10)
- decorative-edge scissors
- copier or scanner

Imagine a nursery where baby is continually looked over by generations of family members. This glowing chandelier doubles as a light fixture and an ethereal display of aunts, uncles, parents, grandparents, and siblings when they were children.

Transparent faces peer through individual crystals that are embellished with old pieces of family jewelry, ribbons, and flowers. Heritage art has never been so dazzling and so lighthearted.

With a nod to the tradition of family members coming together to make a quilt, this project could become a treasured heirloom even before it is presented to the newest family member. Whether you create this meaningful masterpiece by yourself or with others, the first step is to put out a call for photographs. Vintage photos of babies from the Clip Art section can also be used.

If the task of making enough crystals for an entire chandelier seems overwhelming, start with just enough crystals to complete a smaller item to decorate the nursery. Consider using crystals on a wall sconce, dangling from the bottom of a lamp shade or on the bottom of ribbons tied to a drapery rod. Their curvaceous, multifaceted surfaces will sparkle, shimmer, and reflect light no matter where you hang them.

Safety Measures

1 If you are using a vintage or antique chandelier, have it rewired and tested by a professional electrician before using.

2 For all chandeliers, always use the lowest-wattage chandelier lights available.

3 Do not leave the lights on overnight.

4 Use caution in placing paper near the bulbs.

Making the Crystals (see detail shot, top, page 97)

1 Using a photocopier or scanner, size baby family photographs so that the faces fit underneath a chandelier crystal. Once they are sized, print them onto acetate transparency paper.

2 Using the crystal shape as your guide, place the crystal over the baby image on your transparency and cut around the crystal using a craft knife.

3 Use drops of Diamond Glaze around the outside edge of your transparency image to adhere it to the flat side of the crystal. Be sure the crystal is clean and free of fingerprints before you attach the image.

4 Embellish the crystal with rhinestones, old bits of family jewelry, a gold leafing pen along the edge, or foil. These treatments help add character and age to the crystal as though it had been a part of your chandelier for years!

5 You can use the metal hardware that comes with your crystals or you may want to add a new hanging device made from wire or jump rings to attach the crystal to your chandelier.

6 For crystals without imagery, you can use glass paint to give them color and create an antique look with a foiled edge using foil glue and metallic foil sheets.

Making the Chain (bottom, right)

1 Make photocopies of the book page found in the Clip Art section on page 111.

2 Cut the page into strips measuring $3/4$" × $8 1/2$" (1.9 × 21.6 cm).

3 Glue the ends of the strips together to create a chain.

Making the Flowers (bottom, left)

1 Cut a piece of construction paper to measure 9" × 5" (22.9 × 12.7 cm). (The size may need to be adjusted to fit your chandelier.)

2 Fold the paper in half horizontally to measure $4 1/2$" × 5" (11.4 × 12.7 cm) when folded. The folded edge is the top.

3 Draw a horizontal line across the paper 1" (2.5 cm) from the bottom.

4 Cut at $1/4$" (6 mm) intervals from the fold to the line you drew in the previous step. After cutting, wrap the paper around the bottom of the candle part of the chandelier and make a pencil mark where the edges overlap. Cut the paper on the mark.

5 Adhere the sides of the paper (where they overlap at the bottom of the candle) with double-sided adhesive. Use the leftover section of paper for the next candle and then repeat cutting the paper as needed for the remaining candles.

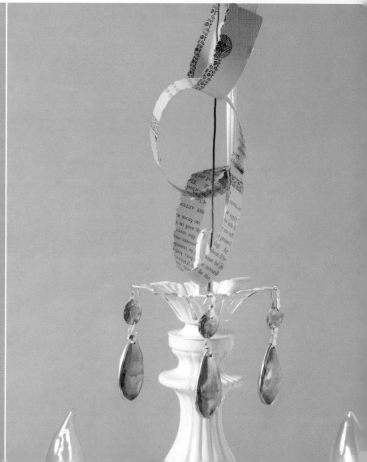

All That Sparkles

Chandeliers were originally candleholders and were hung from the ceiling to illuminate a room and reduce the risk of fire. In the seventeenth century, glass became easy to produce and was hand-cut and polished into different shapes and angles to increase the candlelight power. Achieving this magical effect of reflected light is now a matter of flipping a light switch to turn on a chandelier.

No longer are chandeliers limited to grand ballrooms, palatial estates, or historic buildings. You can pick one up at national chain stores or online in our "good design at any price" era. Put a chandelier in the hands of an interior designer and it becomes a tasteful home décor element. Put it in the hands of a mixed-media artist and it becomes a light fixture that is also a hybrid hip/heritage piece of art.

The Mixed Mediums recall that their first encounter with chandelier crystals occurred when an entire block of antique stores in Newport Beach, California, opened their doors and lured them to an annual event with tasty refreshments and tastier sale prices. One store displayed a large urn full of individual crystals and, although Linda had to put down her complimentary glass of champagne to examine them, there was no question that it was love at first sight—or sip in this case.

The Mediums spent the next year experimenting with coloring the crystals, turning them into embellished brooches and pendants to wear as a necklace. Backing the crystals with acrylic transparencies printed with images of the Eiffel Tower and floral motifs added another dimension. Linda showed the national TV audience how to make jewelry from chandelier crystals on the DIY Network, and soon after that, the Mediums were teaching classes locally and at artists' retreats out of state.

Jenn's dinner order was once held hostage when she wore her exquisite Eiffel Tower Crystal necklace to a favorite restaurant. The waiter was so impressed, he made Jenn promise to make one for his fiancée before he would serve her macadamia nut–encrusted halibut. Actually, he wanted to buy it on the spot but negotiations resulted in the "fish for jewelry" resolution.

Chandeliers can be found at antique fairs and shows and flea markets; see the Resources beginning on page 123 for online resources for purchasing new crystals.

OPPOSITE, TOP

*Vintage crystals mix well with new ones even though you will notice subtle differences in the shapes and the edges. We think the small nicks and scratches add character. This grouping of vintage pieces includes a colonial crystal (**a**), crystal with a pressed flower affixed to the back (**b**), crystal with an amber color wash (**c**), crystal with an unusual shape (**d**), and a teardrop crystal (**e**).*

OPPOSITE, MIDDLE

French pendant crystals come in the following sizes: 1 1/2", 2", 2 1/2", and 3" (3.8, 5.1, 6.4, and 7.6 cm).

Samples of French crystals are shown in their actual size: 3", 2 1/2", and 2" (7.6, 6.4, and 5.1 cm).

The angel crystal is 2" (5.1 cm). Measurements do not include the octagonal bead attached to the top.

OPPOSITE, BOTTOM

You will need crystals that are flat on the back in order to affix transparent photos or pressed flowers. Remove the top bead and replace it when you are finished decorating the crystal. These samples are all 3" (7.6 cm) and show the following techniques: (from left to right) decoupaged flowers with a painted edge and ribbon, butterfly transparency with foil on the back, butterfly transparency with text and a blue painted edge, pressed fern with silver foil edge.

a   b   c   d   e

Leftovers
Quick Ideas for Using Your Scraps

1

A Touch of Glass

Whether you find a few old chandelier crystals at a flea market or purchase new ones online, their faceted glass and lovely shapes make them a perfect choice for holiday decorations or gifts. This one commemorates baby's first Christmas and could also be personalized with a name and a date of birth.

① Select an appropriate size and font and computer generate the text on paper or an acetate transparency.

② Use the crystal as a template and trace the shape onto the printed paper.

③ Affix paper to the back of the crystal with adhesive glue dots.

④ Tie a bow on top and add embellishments if desired.

New Twist on the Old Key Ring

We used leftover baby-themed paper to construct this learning tool to keep baby occupied.

① Cut two pieces of acetate transparency or clear plastic to measure 2" × 3" (5.1 × 7.6 cm). These will be the front and back.

② Punch a hole in the center, near the top.

③ Use the acrylic rectangle as a template to cut paper to the same size.

④ Cut paint chips in various colors or photos and add them to the collection.

2

3

Capsule Container

No need to take along an entire box of baby wipes when baby goes to dinner with the family. Handy plastic capsules or small boxes are available at stores specializing in containers and storage products. A collection of these 4" (10 cm)-high capsules filled with various baby supplies would be a much-appreciated shower gift!

1. Affix printed contact paper around the top of the capsule.

2. Cut printed acetate transparency to fit the circumference of the capsule and affix to one side with adhesive glue dots.

Studio Tip

All three of our Leftovers remind us of the cooking show where they feature meals composed of 70 percent purchased food items and 30 percent homemade. We do the same thing with products from stores, but our recipes combine art materials and paper instead of edible ingredients.

Look for generic items such as tin buckets, photo frames, blank books, lamp shades, wall plaques, or storage containers. Not only can you transform these items into something for baby, you can personalize each one with colors from the nursery, names, birth dates, and photographs.

Make it a habit to consider, "what could I add to that item?" no matter what kind of store you are in. If you shop online, type in "personalize baby" for ideas on bibs, piggy banks, and room décor.

Need more inspiration? Check out www.drooz.com and www.annabelleaustin.com.

TEMPLATES

Any template can be used at the size provided or resized to suit your project's needs—or your artistic eye.

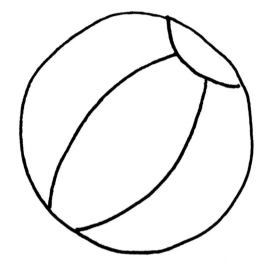

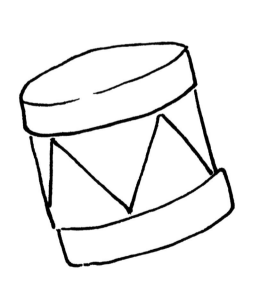

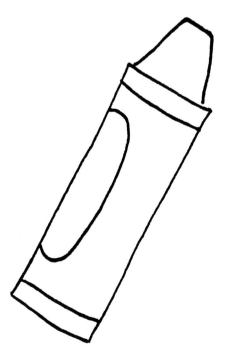

Chinese Take-Out Box Template (page 34)
Photocopy at 133%

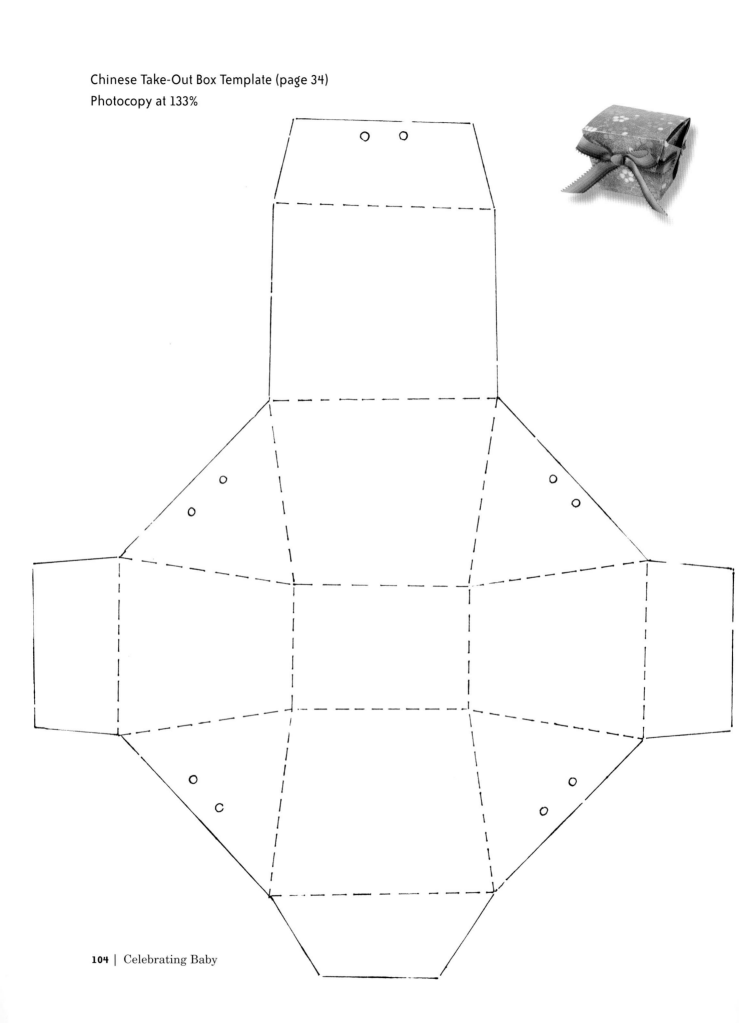

Luggage Tag Template (page 48)
Actual size

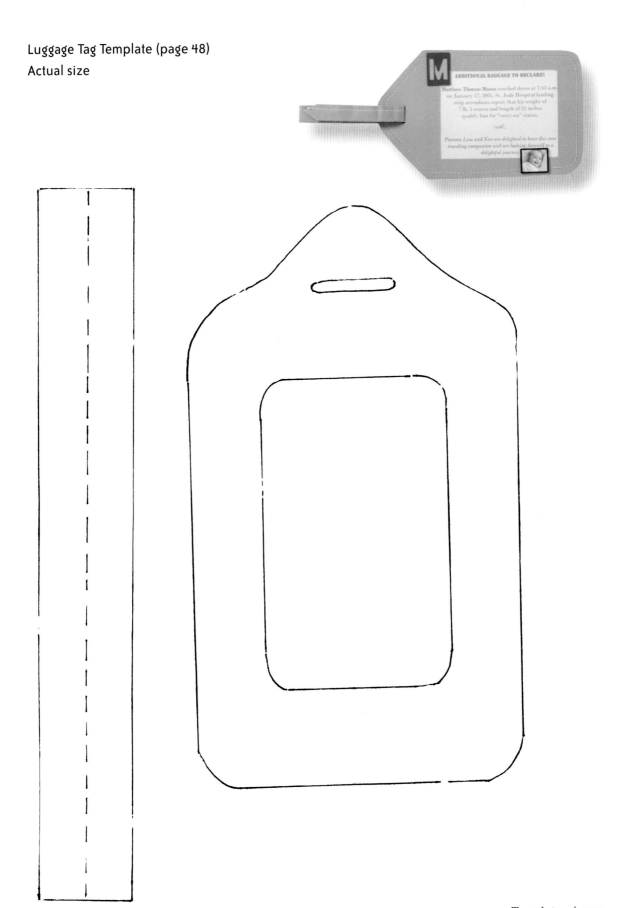

Brag Books Template (page 58)

Growth Chart Height Marking Tab (page 91)

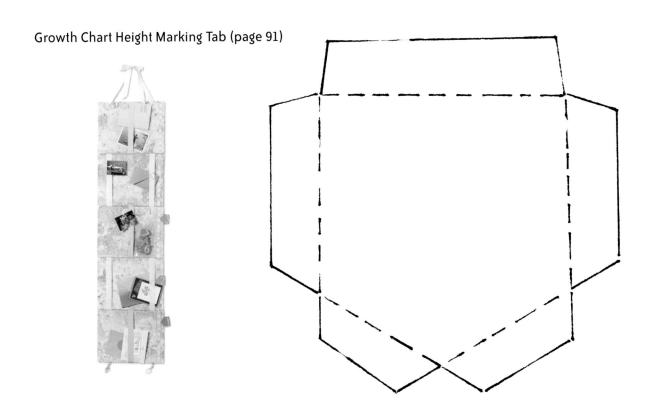

Birthday Blower Template (page 80)

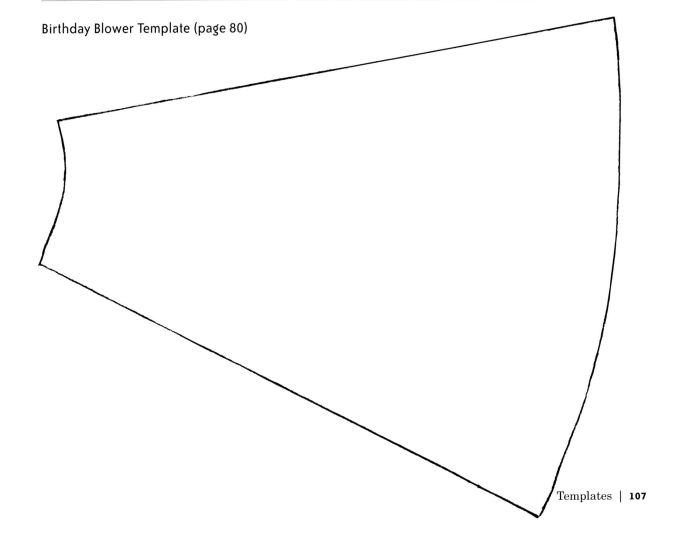

Birthday Hat Template (page 80)
Photocopy at 133%

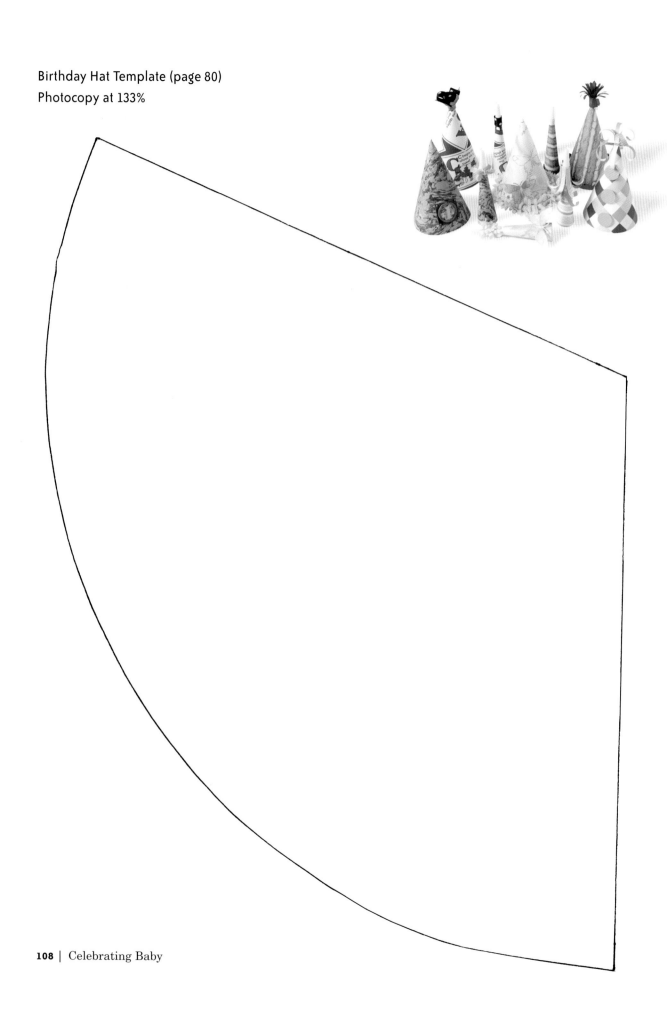

Bib Template (page 79)

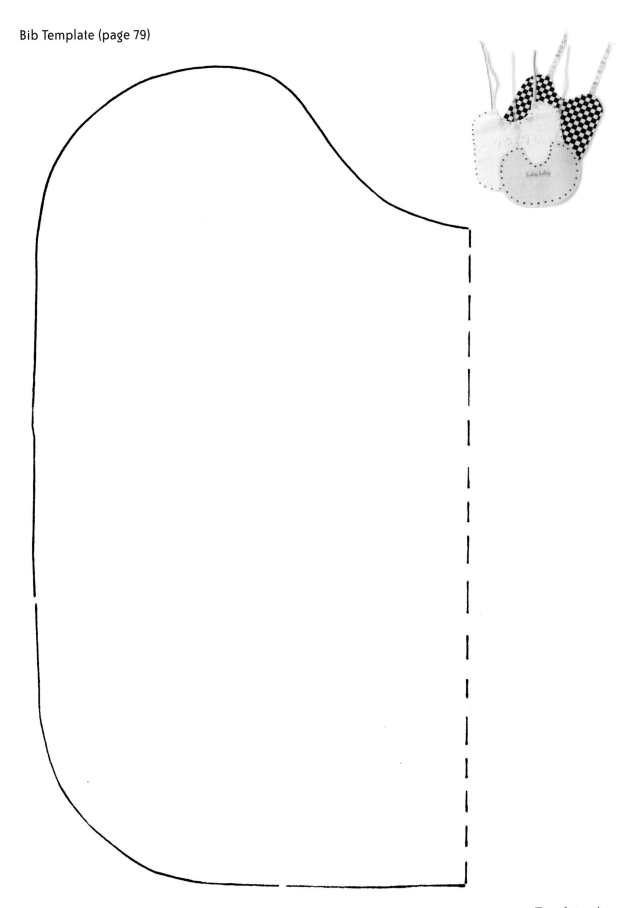

CLIP ART

96   *OUR LANGUAGE*

SECTION 72

Paragraphs

You have noticed that the two letter models (Sections 62 and 64) were divided into paragraphs; that all the sentences in any one paragraph told something about the same subject or topic; that the first line of each paragraph was indented. See if the same facts are true of the following story:

The Wind and the Sun

The Wind and the Sun had a dispute as to which of the two was the stronger. To settle the dispute, they agreed that each should try his strength on a traveler who was walking along the road. The one that could make him take off his coat was to be considered the stronger.

The Wind, who was to try his powers first, puffed himself up, and flew across the field toward the road. He whistled through the fence and blew against the traveler with all his might. Instead of making him take off his coat, however, he wrapped it more closely about him and walked on. The Wind soon gave up in despair.

It was now the Sun's turn to try his strength. As the traveler stepped from beneath the shade of some trees that bordered the road, he felt the burning rays of the Sun beating down upon him. He loosened his coat, and soon took it off and threw it across his arm.

How many paragraphs in this story? What is the first one about? the second? the third? How many lines are indented? Which are they?

Sweetie Pie: (swētē´ pī). *Noun.* **1.** a tot with a sweet disposition. **2.** a little squirt capable of stealing hearts. **3.** all that is lovable and good.

Lovebug: (lŭv´ bŭg). *Noun.* **1.** a small bundle of gurgling joy. **2.** a wee one who is of a darling nature and adorable countenance. **3.** a beloved child.

Cupcake: (cŭp´ cāk). *Noun.* **1.** an engaging moppet. **2.** a small tyke full of wonder and delight. **3.** a small child possessed by an almost edible sweetness.

Sweetie Pie

Cupcake

Love Bug

Calendar

Carriages

Embroidery Edging

Stitching Sample

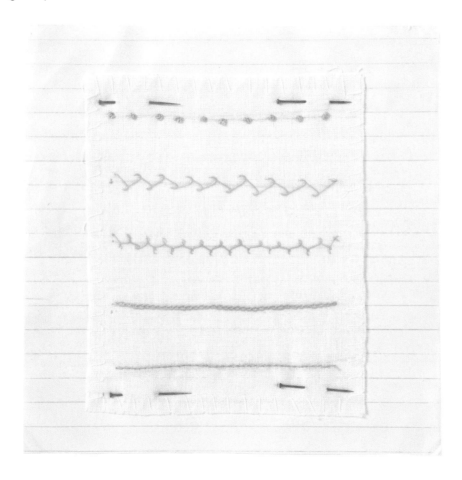

Vintage rulers

Announcement

From: _____
_____
_____
_____

To: _____
_____
_____
_____

THE HEATH PAINT COMPANY

Vintage French Birth Certificate

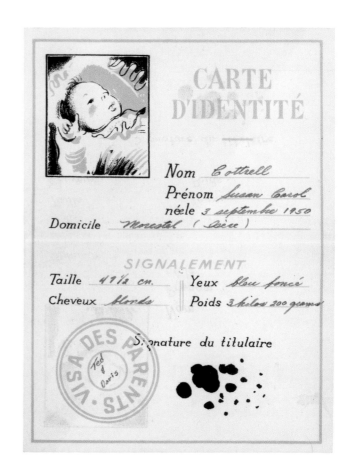

Nursery Page

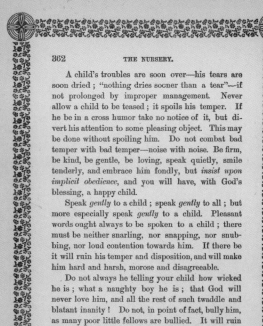

Dictionary Page

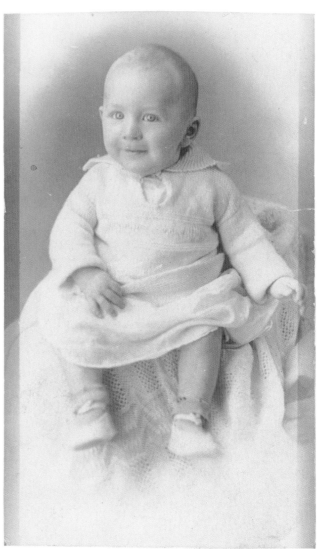

PRODUCT MANUFACTURERS BY PROJECT

Page 15, Around and Around: Repurposed Mobile
canvases, purchased baby mobile, handmade paper, vintage book pages, card stock (Prism Papers), acrylic glazes (Golden), ribbon, black drawing pen, nail heads, soft gel matte (Golden), grommet (Dritz), screw eye hooks, long-reach 1/2" (1.3 cm) circle punch, paintbrush, grommet setter (Dritz), hammer

Page 19, Très Bon: French Flash Cards
card stock or poster board, rub-on letters, chipboard letters (Heidi Swapp), die-cut letters, wooden letters, alphabet stickers (Creative Imaginations), embellishments, wood hearts (Provo Craft), ribbon or twill, linen twine, old French dictionary, cotton fabric paper (Michael Miller Memories), scrapbook paper (Creative Imaginations), tissue paper, zipper, glue stick, adhesive dots, ink pads (Tsukineko), white acrylic paint, black solvent ink stamp, double-sided tape, foam board (Fome-Cor), small key chain, papier-mâché box, spray paint, round corner punch, alphabet die-cut system (QuicKutz)

Page 22, Defining Wall Art: Sweetie Pie Frame
wooden frame, child's flatware, plastic saucer or small plate, stir rods, pie template, die-cut letters, rub-on letters, ribbon, acrylic paint, gesso, watercolor pencils, tissue paper, decorative paper, card stock, white glue, strong adhesive (GOOP), foam tape (3M), decoupage medium/acrylic gel, ink pads (Tsukineko), thick embossing powder, rubber stamp, foam brush, decorative-edge scissors (Fiskars)

Page 25, Beribboned Baby: Hanging Paper Frames
photo, card stock (Prism Papers), decorative paper, acetate (3M), brads, ribbon, decorative-edge scissors (Fiskars)

Page 28, The Art of Letters: ABC Canvas
stretched canvas, chipboard letters in a variety of fonts and sizes (Heidi Swapp, Basic Grey), rub-on letters (Creative Imaginations), decorative paper, sheet music, old ledger pages, or other ephemera (Anna Griffin), velvet flower, felt, skeleton key, ladybug charm, cloth tag (Creative Imaginations), buckle (Creative Imaginations), ribbon (May Arts), gesso (Liquitex), acrylic paint (Delta), crackling medium (Golden), molding paste (Golden), hot glue gun and glue, Sharpie pen, paintbrush, foam brushes, rubber comb, stencils (Wordsworth)

Page 31, Time for Something Sweet: Cupcake Shower
shrink plastic (Lucky Squirrel), card stock (Bazzil), mesh paper (Magenta), decorative paper (Doodlebug Design), brads (Karen Foster Design), ribbon (May Art), acrylic paints (Delta), paintbrush, pigment inks (Yasumoto—Colorcube), black permanent marker (Sharpie), Diamond Glaze (Judi-Kins)

Page 34, Year of the Baby: Chinese Shower
card stock (Prism Papers), decorative paper (Far and Away), eyelets, ribbon (May Arts), chopsticks, markers (EK Success), foam adhesive squares (3M)

Page 39, The Wonder Months: Pregnancy Journal
decorative paper (SEI), card stock (Prism Papers), black Bristol board, chipboard letters and numbers (Provo Craft), eyelets (American Tag Co.), envelopes, ribbon (May Arts), metal label holder (Making Memories), black marker, brads (Making Memories), photo turns, heavy-duty hole punch (American Tag Co.), large corner rounder punch (EK Success), decorative-edge scissors (Fiskars)

Page 48, Tag That Bag: Accessories and Announcements
luggage tag holders (Staples, The Container Store, Michael's), acetate transparencies (3M), decorative papers, adhesive glue dots or tape, alphabet rub-ons or stickers (Creative Imaginations), ribbon (May Arts), embellishments, hook and loop fastener (Velcro)

Page 52, Groundbreaking: Paint Can Announcement
pint-sized paint can (The Container Store), spray paint (Rust-Oleum), label, ribbon (May Arts), coin envelope (Creative Imaginations), charms, card stock (Prism Papers), decorative paper or old blueprints (Karen Foster Designs), adhesive (Aleene's Decoupage Medium), foam tape (3M), postage baby stickers (Pebbles, Inc)

Page 54, A Charmed Life: Photo Memory Bracelet
flat crystal beads with predrilled holes (Auntie's Beads), jump rings, beading wire, crimp beads, assortment of silver decorative spacer beads, assortment of beads, shank-style buttons, small black-and-white photocopied or laser-printed photos, soft gel (Golden), needle-nose pliers, paintbrush, towel, needle tool or awl

Page 56, Proud Daddy Gear: Travel Frame
card stock (Prism Papers), cardboard collectible coin holders, decorative papers (Basic Grey), snaps (American Tag Co.), ink (Tsukineko), glue stick (3M), silicone craft sheet (Ranger Industries), snap setter (American Tag Co.), craft iron, water mister bottle

Page 58, Bragging Rights: Brag Books
mat board, card stock (Prism Papers), decorative paper, metal frame (Making Memories), ribbon, rickrack (Making Memories), foam tape (3M), binder clips or oversized rubber band

Page 63, Memory Valise: Customized Keepsake Suitcase
purchased cardboard suitcase (The Container Store), decorative paper (Cavallini), card stock (Prism Papers), vellum (Prism Papers), mat board, small papier-mâché boxes, tin, ribbon (May Arts), eyelets, round metal-rimmed stationery tags with jump rings, paint, glue stick (3M), bookbinder's cloth or gaffer's tape

Page 67, Big Boy Baby Book: A Grand Tribute to Baby
large-format book, foam board (Fome-Cor), decorative papers, buttons, batting, chenille fabric, rickrack, ephemera, family photos, colored duct tape, ruler tape, metal clips, rub-ons (Creative Imaginations), acetate transparencies (3M), jewel case, adhesive-backed CD envelopes, colored portfolios, newborn clothing items, spray adhesive (3M), E6000 glue, adhesive dots (Therm O Web), double-sided tape (3M), gesso (Golden), quilt basting spray (June Tailor), sewing machine

Page 77, Dining in Style: Totes, Bibs, and Place Mats
decorative paper, contact paper (Rubbermaid), table cover (Costco), gift bags, ribbon, clear container tube, cardboard container tube, acetate transparency (3M), clear plastic tubing, small beads, Lucite purse handle, disposable plastic forks and spoons, adhesive-backed CD holder, plastic sleeve, small book, glue stick (3M), spray adhesive (3M), adhesive dots (Therm O Web)

Page 80, Party Time! Birthday Hats and Blowers
watercolor paper (Strathmore), shimmery watercolors (US ArtQuest), ink, kosher or coarse salt, tissue paper, noisemakers removed from generic party blowers, adhesive foam squares (3M), $1/4$" (6 mm)-wide industrial-strength tape, ribbon or elastic (May Arts), paintbrush, stamp (Just for Fun), sewing machine

Page 84, It's All Relative: A Book about Family
child's board book, decorative paper (My Mind's Eye), charms (Boutique Trims), ribbon (May Arts, Offray), card stock (Prism Papers), QuicKutz alphabet, rub-on letters (Making Memories), frames (Making Memories), metal clips (7gypsies), oval sticker (K & Co.), epoxy stickers (Creative Imaginations), photographs, mounting foam tape (3M), adhesive (Aleene's Decoupage Medium), decorative-edge scissors (Fiskars), Sharpie pen

Page 88, Ten Minutes to Orange: Paint Chip Clock
round clock, paint chips in a rainbow of colors, color wheel, small square wooden blocks (Walnut Hollow), adhesive-backed numbers, clock hands (7gypsies)

Page 92, Climbing Jacob's Ladder: Growth Chart and Memo Board
card stock (Prism Papers), canvas art boards (Frederix), dish soap, acrylic paint (Golden, Making Memories), soft gel (Golden), ribbon (May Arts), ruler clip art, heavy-duty hole punch (American Tag Co.), number stamps (Hot Potato)

Page 95, Let There Be Light: Heritage Chandelier
acetate transparency (3M), chandelier (or sconce, lamp shade, etc), colored card stock (Prism Papers), photographs, embellishments for crystals, glass paint, foil (Jones Tones), foil glue (Aileen's), pages from a vintage children's book, Diamond Glaze (Judi-Kins), crystals or pendants (Freedom Crystal), thin wire or jump rings, glue stick or glue dots (3M or Therm O Web), flame-retardant spray (Flamex, National Fireproofing Co.)

OUT AND ABOUT WITH THE MIXED MEDIUMS

During the process of writing *Celebrating Baby,* the Mixed Mediums realized there were times when we had to close our laptops, peel the gel medium off our fingers, and hit the road for a field trip. These are some of the stores that enchanted, excited, and inspired us. Many are small, one-of-a-kind places where you can chat with the owners about their merchandise, art philosophy, and nearby restaurants for lunch. Others are large, national stores that may not be as cozy and personal but offer dazzling displays and the latest in innovative paper goods. Either way, it is all about the experience of shopping as much as it is about acquiring materials.

With a few clicks on your computer, you can take a look at our favorite stores from tiny towns on the California coast, to the boulevards of Paris and the winding side streets of Florence. The larger, nationwide stores have catalogs. Order one when you visit the website and you will be delighted each time a copy shows up in your mailbox.

Resources

UNITED STATES

Annabelle Austin & Company: *Wholesale design firm specializing in handmade gifts and keepsakes*
www.annabelleaustin.com

Anthropologie: *a nationwide home accessories and clothing store that always incorporates paper art in its merchandising displays. Quirky, clever, and always something new*
www.anthropologie.com

Archiver's: *lovely memory, scrapbook, and paper art stores throughout the Midwest*
www.archiversonline.com

The ARTbar: *mixed-media art studio and retail store in an exquisite historical building*
Santa Ana, CA
714.558.2445
www.theartbar.net

babystyle: *maternity, baby and kids clothing, accessories, and gifts. Stores nationwide*
www.babystyle.com

drooz studio: *website offering handpainted hangings, plaques, and more*
www.drooz.com

French General: *elegant ephemera, antique buttons, notions, beads and ribbon—all fromantique fairs in the south of France*
Hollywood, CA
323.462.0818
www.frenchgeneral.com

Hobby Lobby Creative Centers: *general crafts and hobby supplies*
www.hobbylobby.com

Horchow: *chandeliers, sconces, and other lighting options in many price ranges*
www.horchow.com

Jennifer Price Studio: *an ever-changing assemblage of handcrafted functional art*
At SoLo in Solana Beach, CA
858.794.9016
www.jenniferpricestudio.com

Jo-Ann Stores: *fabrics and crafts and all the basics*
www.joann.com

Kate's Paperie: *beautiful paper boutique with locations around New York City*
www.katespaperie.com

Lucky Paperie: *letterpress designs, journals, memory books, albums, and paper*
Pasadena, CA
626.440.9440
www.luckypaperie.com

Michael's: *national chain of craft and art supply stores—where to go to find the basics*
800.MICHAELS
www.michaels.com

Paper Source: *these stores throughout the United States are a delight for paper lovers. We spend hours looking at the books, display samples, and handmade papers. Request their catalog when you check out the website*
www.paper-source.com

Paperie: *a sumptuous assortment of handmade papers and journals*
San Diego, CA
619.234.5457

Paris to the Moon: *paper artists reign in this store that is like stepping back in time to the Victorian era*
Costa Mesa, CA
949.642.0942

For a preview of their magical merchandise visit:
www.studiodsharp.com
www.fgandcompany.com

Pottery Barn Kids: *unique collection of toys, furniture, accessories, and gifts for babies and children*
www.potterybarnkids.com

ReCollections: *Michael's-owned stores devoted to papercraft and scrapbooking*
www.recollectionsonline.com

Ruby Lang: *antiquities, oddities, and wearable paper extravaganzas*
At SoLo in Solana Beach, CA
858.794.9016

Sterling Art: *another paper paradise for excellent art supplies and museum-quality paper for replicating artwork*
800.953.2953
www.sterlingart.com

Target: *design for the masses, and lovely supplies for paper art and more*
www.target.com

Urban Outfitters: *chandeliers, sconces, and other lighting options in many price ranges*
www.urbanoutfitters.com

Resources for new crystals
www.chandelierparts.com
www.cristalier.com
www.freedomcrystal.com

INTERNATIONAL RESOURCES

Australia
Eckersley's Arts, Crafts, and Imagination
(store locations in New South Wales, Queensland, South Australia, and Victoria)
phone for catalog: 61.1.300.657.766
www.eckersleys.com.au

Canada
Curry's Art Store
Ontario
art and craft supplies
800.268.2969
www.currys.com

Lazar Studiowerx Inc
British Columbia
rubber stamps, art tools
866.478.9379
www.lazarstudiowerx.com

France
Jen Bitto has spent hours researching paper stores in Paris and allotted an entire day to check them out. Take an armchair vacation to the City of Lights by visiting the websites provided showing Jen's favorite shops.

Calligrane
4-6 Rue du Pont Louis Phillipe
Paris

Graphigro
art supplies
6e arrondissement
133, Rue de Rennes
Paris
www.graphigro.com
33.01.53.36000

L'Art du Papier
48 Rue Vavin
Paris
www.art-du-papier.fr

Marie Papier
26 Rue Vavin
Paris
www.mariepapier.com

Papier +
9 Rue du Pont Louis Philippe
Paris
www.papierplus.com

Italy
Italians have been making the world's most beautiful paper for hundreds of years. Perhaps that is why they don't feel the need to establish websites! These are Linda's favorite paper stores in Florence. They may not be on the Web but you will find them all within walking distance of the Duomo.

Carteria Tassotti, Via Dei Servi 9/11r
Rome

Et Cetera, Via Della Vigna Nuova 82/r
Rome

Il Papiro, Via Cavour, 55r
Rome

Rigacci, Via Dei Servi 7
Rome

And, when in Rome, spend some time at Fabriano, the famous Italian paper company. They actually have a well-stocked and beautiful store at the Rome airport, of all places. This is a paper aficionado's idea of what every airport should offer at the departure gates!

New Zealand
Littlejohns Art & Graphic Supplies Ltd.
170 Victoria Street
Wellington
64.04.385.2099

United Kingdom
Creative Crafts
11 The Square
Winchester,
Hampshire SO23 9ES
44.01962.856266
www.creativecrafts.co.uk

HobbyCraft Group Limited
7 Enterprise Way
Aviation Park
Bournemouth International Airport
Christchurch
Dorset BH23 6HG
44.01202.596100
www.hobbycraft.co.uk
Arts and crafts supplies

John Lewis
(stores throughout the UK)
Flagship Store
Oxford Street
London W1A 1EX
44.01207.629 7711
www.johnlewis.co.uk

T. N. Lawrence & Son Ltd.
208 Portland Road
Hove BN3 5QT
44.0845.644.3232
www.lawrence.co.uk

FLEA MARKETS AND ANTIQUE SHOWS
www.brimfieldshow.com
Jenn Mason's yearly trek to the famous Brimfield Antique and Collectible in Brimfield, Massachusetts, has become a tradition that garners her one-of-a-kind embellishments, ephemera, and a chance to spend the day with her East Coast girlfriends.

www.discoverfrance.net
Listing of France's best flea markets

www.fleamarketguide.com
State-by-state markets in the United States

www.shortcitybreak.co.uk
European flea markets locator

Product Resources

Website and/or contact information is provided below for products used in this book. Many of these company websites either allow you to order directly (and ship internationally) or list stores where their products are available.

3M
www.3M.com
Adhesives including glue sticks, specialty tapes, foam tape squares, and spray adhesives. Also transparencies and laminating supplies

7gypsies
www.7gypsies.com
Scrapbooking supplies including unusual embellishments

Aleene's
www.duncancrafts.com
adhesives and crafting supplies

American Tag Co.
www.americantag.net
HomePro tool for hole punching and setting snaps, eyelets, rivets, metal corners, clock hands, nail heads, and rhinestones

Anna Griffin, Inc.
www.annagriffin.com
Fine decorative paper and embellishments for scrapbooking and paper arts

Avery
www.avery.com
Office tags and supplies

Carta Products
www.cartaproducts.com
Colored pencil sets

Basic Grey
www.basicgrey.com
Specialty scrapbooking papers

Bazzil Basics Paper, Inc.
www.bazzillbasics.com
Card stock, paper products, and embellishments for scrapbooking

Cavallini
www.cavallini.com
Fine Italian decorative papers and accessories

The Container Store
www.thecontainerstore.com
Organizational supplies and gift wrap

Costco
www.costco.com
Superstore for home goods

Creative Imagination
www.cigift.com
Scrapbook papers, supplies, and embellishments

Delta Crafts
www.deltacrafts.com
Paint and crafting supplies

Doodlebug Design Inc.
www.doodlebug.ws
Paper, ribbon, and embellishments for scrapbooking

Dritz
www.dritz.com
Sewing, quilting and craft supplies

EK Success
www.eksuccess.com
Scrapbook papers, supplies, and embellishments

Fancifuls, Inc.
www.fancifulsinc.com
Brass charms and embellishments

Far and Away
www.farandawayscrapbooks.com
Decorative scrapbook papers

Fiskars
www.fiskars.com
www.fiskarscrafts.com
Scissors and cutting implements

Flamex
www.natfire.com/flame.retardant_fx.htm
Flame-retardant spray for paper (from the National Fireproofing Company)

Freedom Crystal
www.freedomcrystal.com
Crystal chandeliers and parts

GOOP
www.eclecticproducts.com
Do-it-yourself adhesives and products

Golden
www.goldenpaints.com
Quality line of paints, fluid acrylics, and mediums for art

Heidi Swapp
www.heidiswapp.com
Decorative scrapbook paper and embellishments

Hot Potato
www.hotpotatoes.com
Products for stamping and heat embossing on velvet

Jones Tones
www.jonestones.com
Manufacturer of paints, glues, glitters, foils, arts and crafts, and other decorating products

Judi-Kins
www.judikins.com
Stamps and supplies, including Diamond Glaze

Karen Foster Design
www.karenfosterdesign.com
Scrapbook papers and embellishments

Krylon
www.krylon.com
Paints and painting products

Liquitex
www.liquitex.com
Fine-art paint, gels, mediums, and supplies

Lowe's
www.lowes.com
Hardware supplies

Lucky Squirrel
www.luckysquirrel.com
Shrink plastic supplies

Magenta
www.art-of-craft.co.uk
Stamps and stamping supplies

Making Memories
www.makingmemories.com
Scrapbook paper, tools, supplies, and embellishments

May Arts
www.mayarts.com
Ribbons for crafts and decorating

Michael Miller Memories
www.michaelmillermemories.com
Fabric scrapbook and craft paper

Michael's
www.michaels.com
Craft supplies

Norcom, Inc.
www.norcominc.com
Mini composition books

Paper Source
www.paper-source.com
Paper for paper art and scrapbooking

Prism
www.prismpapers.com
Large selection of fine card stocks for paper crafting including exclusive textured line

Provo Craft
www.provocraft.com
Craft supplies

QuicKutz
www.quickutz.com
Die-cut machine and unique alphabet and shaped dies

ReadySet
www.readysettools.com
Unique eyelet setting tool that can be used anywhere

Rubbermaid
www.rubbermaid.com
Plastic storage and Con-Tact paper

Rust-Oleum
www.rustoleum.com
Specialty paints

Sanford
www.sanford.com
Sharpie markers

Scrapworks
www.scrapworks.com
Scrapbook paper, tools, supplies, and embellishments

SEI
www.shopsei.com
Scrapbook paper and supplies

Staples
www.staples.com
Office and paper supplies

Swingline
www.swingline.com
Staplers and supplies

Therm O Web
www.thermoweb.com
Adhesive (Zots)

Tsukineko
www.tsukineko.com
Fine-quality inks and ink pads for your crafting projects.

X-Acto
www.hunt-corp.com
Craft knives and blades

Velcro
www.velcro.com
Hook and loop tape

Walnut Hollow
www.walnuthollow.com
Wood, wood turnings, and tools

Wordsworth
www.wordsworthstamps.com
Stamps, stickers, papers, and templates

Supply Contributors

Special thanks to the following manufacturers for contributing their products for use in this book. We encourage you to look into these companies and their wonderful products.

3M
St. Paul, MN 55144 USA
888.3M.HELPS (364.3577)
www.3m.com
All-purpose arts, crafts, and office supplies

American Tag Co.
800.223.3956
www.americantag.net
Manufacturer of the HomePro heavy-duty hole punch, and eyelet, rivet, nail head, metal corner, snap, and rhinestone setter

Anna Griffin Inc.
733 Lambert Drive
Atlanta, GA 30324 USA
888.817.8170
www.annagriffin.com
Scrapbook papers and embellishments

Cavallini
401 Forbes Boulevard
South San Francisco, CA 94080 USA
800.226.5287
www.cavalinni.com
Paper products

The C-Thru Ruler Company
6 Britton Drive
Bloomfield, CT 06002 USA
800.243.8419
www.cthruruler.com
Cutting-edge innovator and international leader in measurement and art materials

Fiskars
2537 Daniels Street
Madison, WI 53718 USA
866.348.5661
www.fiskars.com
www.fiskarscrafts.com
High-quality, reliable craft tools and supplies

Golden
188 Bell Road
New Berlin, NY 13411-9527 USA
800.959.6543
www.goldenpaints.com
Professional-quality art materials that extend creative opportunities for artists and strengthen industry standards

Heidi Swapp
Advantus Corporation
12276 San Jose Boulevard
Building 115
Jacksonville, FL 32223 USA
904.482.0092
www.heidiswapp.com
Scrapbook papers and embellishments

May Arts
203.637.5285 (fax)
sales@mayarts.com
www.mayarts.com
Beautiful ribbons for crafting, sewing, and decorating

Prism
P O Box 25068
Salt Lake City, UT 84125 USA
866.901.1002
www.prismpapers.com
Scrapbooking papers

QuicKutz, Inc.
1365 West 1250 South
Suite 100
Orem, UT 84058 USA
888.702.1146
www.quickutz.com
Portable, accessible die-cutting

Scrapworks, Inc.
3038 Specialty Circle
Suite C
Salt Lake City, UT 84115 USA
801.363.1010
www.scrapworks.com
Scrapbook papers and embellishments

Tsukineko, Inc
17640 N.E. 65th Street
Redmond, WA 98052 USA
425.883.7733
425.883.7418 (fax)
www.tsukineko.com
Fine-quality inks and inkpads for your crafting projects

ABOUT THE AUTHORS

The Mixed Mediums are Jenn Mason, Linda Blinn, and Jennifer Francis Bitto. The name is a play on their various talents as artists and writers, and also on their passionate interest in creating mixed-media paper art that takes the word *craft* to another level. This is the second book in their Paper Art Workshop series, offering beautiful, clever, fun, and sophisticated ideas for handmade *baby gifts*—all with paper as a common element. Jenn Mason can be contacted through her website, www.JennMason.com.

ACKNOWLEDGMENTS

We extend our greatest gratitude and appreciation to Mary Ann Hall, editor extraordinaire, for her tireless emails ×3 to get the titles just right; for her fabulous font awareness; and for her support helping the Mixed Mediums come to life. Our boundless thanks also go to the Quarry Books staff for their generosity, proofreading, editing, and photography skills. And to our spouses and families, we thank you once again for seeing us through the roller coaster of deadlines, understanding our need to follow inspiration at any time of day, and helping with the dirty dishes.

LOOKING FOR MORE
FROM THE MIXED MEDIUMS' PAPER ART WORKSHOP?

Paper Art Workshop

HANDMADE GIFTS

Stylish Ideas for Journals, Stationery, and More

Let *Handmade Gifts* take you on an inspiring journey into the world of designer paper crafting!

Handmade Gifts, the premier volume in the Paper Art Workshop series, features an exquisite collection of beautiful handmade paper gifts unlike any you have seen before. Each chapter offers ideas for a particular kind of person, such as a traveler, a cook, or a girlfriend. The projects include customized journals, gift books, stylish stationery supplies, paper flowers, paper jewelry, gift tags, and much, much more. Learn simple techniques and expert studio tips that will take your passion for beautiful paper to the next level.